By His Mercy 3: Take Up Your Cross

How 11 Ordinary Young Catholics have
seen God's Extraordinary Mercy

By His Mercy 3: Take Up Your Cross
How 11 Ordinary Young Catholics have seen God's Extraordinary Mercy

Thomas Kleinschnitz
Anna Carmody
Justin Edin
Victoria Hammond
Jared Beumer
Ann Marschel
Morgan Ness
Zach Silbernick
Shannon Hillestad
Michael Haney
Fr. Andrew Vogel

Foreward by Fr. Scott Pogatchnik
Cover by Leah Wheeles
Edited by Nikki Silbernick

Tricia Walz
2021

First Printing: 2021

ISBN: 978-1-716-54540-5

Tricia Walz
Saint Cloud, MN 56303

Cover Artist: Leah Wheeles

Contents

Acknowledgements

I would like to thank everyone for all the love and support throughout this process of the *By His Mercy* series. I can't thank everyone enough. I'd like to give a special thanks to each of the authors who were willing to share such personal stories with the world.

Thank you to my family, especially my beautiful daughter Alesha who has been so supportive of the creation of this book!

I would like to give a special thank you to Nikki Silbernick who helped edit testimonies and to Mark McGowan who helped with the technology. A big thanks as well to Leah Wheeles who painted the beautiful cover.

We would like to thank all the priests and religious who have given their life to the Lord. We are forever grateful for all that you do and are! The proceeds for this series of books goes to the Vocations Office for the Diocese of St. Cloud. Thank you for helping us support the young men and women discerning God's plan for their lives!

God bless you all!
Tricia Walz

"Everything is a reminder of the Cross. We ourselves are made in the shape of a cross."

-Saint John Vianney

Foreword

Heart of Jesus: The Cruciform Shape of Mercy

Greetings and welcome - it's pure joy to introduce to you *By His Mercy 3: Take Up Your Cross*! But please be warned: this rather harmless-looking softcover contains testimonies to Christ's mercy that can open new ways of seeing Jesus Christ and how personally He loves you.

In *By His Mercy 3*, you will find ten individuals from varied backgrounds all describing a God Who never stopped pursuing them. This God took flesh in Jesus Christ and promised, "I will be with you always, until the end of the age" (Mt 28:20). This volume, combined with the 24 testimonies from previous volumes, urges us to consider the closing words of St. John's soaring gospel:

"There are also many other things that Jesus did, but if these were to be described individually, I do not think the whole world would contain the books that would be written" (Jn 21:25).

Though not properly part of Scripture, the following encounters are precisely what St. John describes: a continuation of the gospel in which Jesus is alive and acts through His Holy Spirit. These are "things Jesus did." How could it be otherwise? Again and again, we see Jesus choosing disciples to follow Him, but first asking permission to heal them. "What would you like me to do for you?" Jesus asks. "Isn't it obvious, Lord?" - and yet He waits until He knows it's best.

A helpful illustration of Christ's mercy in action comes through the vocation of Our Holy Father, Pope Francis. A brief sketch of the one-day Pope's encounter will suffice. As high schoolers, Jorge Bergoglio and his classmates would welcome each year the 21st of September - the feast of St. Matthew - as a holiday to celebrate with friends. One year, eager to join his friends for celebrations at the main square, Jorge felt prompted by the Holy Spirit to make a confession. "What are the odds a priest is at the church on a holiday?" he thought. And yet, as he turned the corner to the church, he saw a priest waiting out front who he had never seen before. What's more, Jorge had the real sense that this priest had been there for some time and was truly waiting for him. Overwhelmed with grace, Jorge didn't just make a good confession but encountered a mercy that turned his life to Christ in a way that would mark him forever.

In fact, after being selected as Pope, he chose as his motto *Miserando atque Eligendo* - 'Looking upon Him with Mercy, Christ Chose Him.' These words are taken from St. Bede's commentary on Matthew's conversion - a biblical mercy that Pope Francis found waiting for him in front of a church so many years earlier. I encourage you to read this commentary on your own: you can find it in the Office of Readings on St. Matthew's feast day, September 21st.

More locally, the history of the Diocese of Saint Cloud has seen many others moved by Christ to offer their lives for the Kingdom, whether through regular confession, prayer before the Blessed Sacrament, or an evangelical impulse to bring Christ to the world. Space doesn't permit an account of the lives of Father Francis Xavier Pierz, Sister Adelaide Koetter, Father John Kaiser, or the miraculous healing of Patricia Bitzan that led to the beatification of Blessed Columba Marmion in 2000, but I encourage you to explore them. To meet these saints and martyrs is to meet Christ Himself.

Our world is so obsessed with the self, seeking every angle of self-examination in the pursuit of perfection. The Father's mercy says something very different. It says, "I am the only one who can see you perfectly - so come to Me and let Me tend to your wounds and thus reveal to you the incredible, unrepeatable son or daughter that you truly are. I want you to live from that identity - that the world might know the Face of the Father!"

So again, it is pure joy to recommend these testimonies to you. They come through ten amazing "saints-in-the-making" and yet are truly a continuation of the Life of Christ offered as a gift to all. These disciples have prayed for you as they wrote these words, so have no fear. Christ waits for you, He looks upon you with Mercy, and He chooses you. All He asks is your permission.

In the Mercy of the Father, Son, and Holy Spirit,

Fr. Scott Pogatchnik
Diocese of Saint Cloud
Rector, Pastor, and Vocation Director
December 13, 2020
3rd Sunday of Advent - Gaudete Sunday

Thomas Kleinschnitz

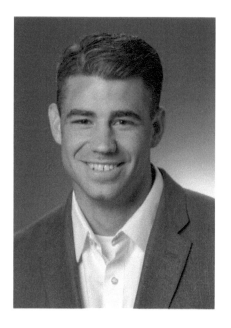

"Every Saint has a past, and every sinner has a future."

-Oscar Wilde

My story starts when I was a young boy. My parents were going through a rough patch in their marriage. They had split apart, and my father was no longer living in our home. I was young enough to where my daily activities and functions were not impacted too greatly, but old enough to know something was wrong. More importantly, I was old enough to feel the strain on our family. There are two main memories from this experience. The first is walking into the living room and witnessing the agony on my mother's face as she was crying into her hands. She had just gotten off the phone with my father. I do not know what the conversation consisted of, but I remember feeling my mother's pain as if it were my own. I distinctly remember telling myself, "I will never cause anyone this much pain." The second memory is my first man-to-man talk with my father. He was dropping me off from hanging out together, and as we pulled into the driveway, I asked him if he was going to be back together with mom in time for Christmas. He paused and took a deep breath, staring at the windshield. I could tell he was trying to gather his thoughts. He eventually looked over at me and said, "Sorry, son; this year Christmas is going to be different." Pausing, trying to gain control of his emotions, he continued, "I need you to do me a favor, Thomas. You are the oldest boy, and with me not at home that makes you the man of the house. I need you to look after your mother and four other siblings for me." His voice began to crack. This was the first time I can remember witnessing my father emotional. My father was the strongest man I knew. He was my hero. Like any boy I imagine having this conversation, I replied, "Okay, I can do that," having no idea of the weight or responsibility that I just accepted. I agreed because I knew my father was hurting and he needed my help. Walking up the driveway, I stopped and turned to wave like usual. Yet, when I saw my father's face embedded into his palms, I felt an overwhelming hurt. I did not know it at the time, but I was witnessing my hero wounded for the first time, and my hurt came from not knowing how to help him.

I started with those two memories because they were my first experiences of woundedness within our family. Even though I did not know it at the time, those encounters had a major impact on my view of faith and family. My parents reconciled after many years of counseling and in the end, they became a much stronger example of union for our family.

As years passed, I began focusing heavily on basketball. It became my outlet and my escape. It was the one place where I could leave all the weight I was carrying at the door. Even though my parents had reconciled, I still felt an internal responsibility to live up to the expectation as man of the house. However, nothing mattered when I was on the basketball court, except how hard I played. Those who were able to watch me play saw how I always left everything on the court, many times literally. It was my way of emptying myself of the frustrations and worries from the world around me. Unfortunately, as I entered high school, basketball by then had become my identity, and that created distance between me and God. This created an opportunity for Satan to work his way into my life. As I focused heavily on playing at the collegiate level, it was easy for me to stay away from drugs and alcohol. Girls, however, proved to be a different story. In my junior year of high school, I lost my virginity to the girl I was dating at the time. Up until that point, I had always told myself and everyone else that I wanted to wait until marriage. My faith growing up was something I leaned on heavily to get through. However, this was the first time in my life where I needed to stand up for what I believed in and failed. I put aside my faith for my own selfishness. Even though we cared very strongly about each other (or at least that was what I told myself to justify my actions), I knew marriage was not an option for us, as our lives were headed in different directions. I tried to bury the feeling the best I could, but deep down I knew I had opened a door that was not ready to be opened. I had made myself a promise after watching my parents struggle all those years that I would wait until marriage so my wife and I could properly fulfill the Sacrament, and I had now broken that promise. I obviously was not paying attention to the severity of the situation, but Satan was. Giving myself away at 17 opened a door for Satan to enter my life.

I was successful at earning a college scholarship for basketball. Attaining that goal serves as a constant reminder that hard work, determination, and never giving up pays off. However, it was during college that I had my darkest years. You would have thought I would be on top of the world, since by my sophomore year I had worked my way to a starting position and was leading the team in just about every statistical category. At our peak, we were ranked 7th in the nation. However, off the court I felt empty and alone. When I got to college, I abandoned the principles and habits that made me successful. Without my family, I was longing for a sense of community. So, I began partying to join the peers around me. It did not take long for Satan to exploit this opportunity and grab ahold of my life at this point. For me, partying led to poor choices, and each poor choice left me feeling more empty and alone than before. Eventually these poor choices started to have an impact on the direction of my life. By the end of my sophomore year in college, I could feel myself slipping into depression. Longing for my family, I decided to go home for the weekend and regather myself. When I was driving back to campus that Sunday evening, I found myself deep in thought and praying to God for guidance. I felt I was losing control of my life, and I needed His help. This led to my first encounter with Christ. The best way for me to describe it is to think of a scene from a movie where the actor's soul comes out of his body. That is what it felt like. During this time, I remember looking to my passenger seat and seeing a light. The light was talking to me. I instantly knew this was God. He told me, "If you give yourself to Me, I will get your life back on track. However, it will not be easy. To fix your wounds, I will need to take you from your two greatest joys: basketball and family." Naturally, as my soul went back into my body and I had this overwhelming wave of emotion, I panicked. I finished my drive back to campus and emailed my father the conversation I just had with God. Over the next few weeks, we discussed, prayed, and discerned the best course of action. Listening to God meant walking away from my college scholarship, something that my father and I had worked excessively hard for, for many years. Ultimately, we believed God would take care of me, so I walked away from my scholarship. I attended a college in Gainesville, Florida, which was roughly three and a half hours away from my family. Being the farthest I had ever been from my family and not playing basketball, I thought this was where God wanted me to be. I was mistaken, because I had attached my own selfishness to the decision of attending school in Gainesville.

My junior year of college, I was in a relationship that started off great but became very toxic. We ignored our differences in exchange for our own selfish desires. There was a saying father would tell me growing up, "men give up love for sex, and woman give up sex for love." This is a perfect depiction of our relationship. We both had deep personal wounds that needed to be focused on, but instead we tried to bury our problems in our own selfish ways. Driven by alcohol and premarital sex, our selfishness ultimately destroyed our relationship. Instead of working to build each other up into better human beings, we pulled each other down. Finally, I was able to muster together enough strength to walk away from the relationship. Or so I thought. Soon after I broke off our relationship, she informed me she was pregnant. That was the moment everything started to fall apart for me. I had turned into the person I promised myself I would never become. Here I was putting a girl through the same level of agony I promised I would never create. Watching her cry was like watching my mother cry many years earlier. Knowing we could never survive as a couple; I knew we would be raising a child in a broken home. The amount of hurt was unbearable. With each day that passed, I could feel myself being torn apart. I began drinking more, and slowly I felt a level of dependency I never had before.

I started praying again, begging for help. God answered my call with a firm yet gentle, "Nice try, Thomas; this time I need you to follow Me on my terms not yours." I started going to Mass again and praying each day, simply asking for strength and guidance. I slowly began to feel as if it would all turn out okay, but that is when I received the most painful news yet. Eight weeks into the pregnancy, she miscarried. Since she was threatening to have an abortion if I did not marry her, I initially felt a sense of relief. That relief was very quickly replaced with a crippling feeling of guilt. The last thing I wanted was for the child to be hurt. My poor life choices were not the baby's fault. Yet, the harsh reality was that a child lost his life because I didn't have the courage or the strength to stand up for what I truly believed in, a tragedy that haunts me to this day. What hurts me the most though, is the knowledge that I had the ability to control my circumstances. However, I continuously gave in to Satan's temptations instead of working hard, dedicating myself, and not giving up on the promises I had made to myself and my future wife.

Up until this point, I had not shared the news about the pregnancy with my family. To them, I was always the second man of the house, the one my siblings could look up to in times of hardship. I did not want to hurt them or our relationship. I was fearful of the disappointment and shame it would bring our family. So, it was a good thing God had reentered my life when He did, because I don't know if I would have been able to take the news of the baby passing alone. As tough as it was, I could feel God with me, and I knew everything would work out if I continued to follow Him. This time, I stayed true to the commitment of following His will.

Going into my fourth year of college, I was trusting in God as He introduced me to Franciscan University of Steubenville, a small Catholic University in Southeast Ohio. I was very hesitant to be so far from my family. Little did I know that God would be introducing me to a new one: a faith-based community that was going to be able to support me on my journey to redemption. Franciscan introduced Catholicism to me on a dynamic level, a level I never knew existed. It was my first-time encountering priests who preached homilies with passion and a genuine desire to share God's message. Spending time getting to know many of the priests and nuns on campus was reassuring for me, because many of the religious had stories like mine. They had a past where they, too, made poor choices that greatly impacted their lives. Now, I have never felt the calling to enter the religious life, but it was comforting to hear others overcome their past. It brought me hope that I could do the same.

Franciscan is where I met students who were just like me, except they were filled with a burning fire to be living witnesses of the

Gospel. At Franciscan, all the students had two things in common: we all had a story, and we all wanted to improve our story by growing in our faith to build a foundation strong enough to challenge the world. Franciscan brought individuals together for one mission: to make this world a better place by building up the Church through community. The University had the goal of teaching us and supporting us along our roads to redemption, so that we could fulfill our greatest potential, becoming the persons God created us to be. Most of us never had any intention of joining the religious life; we just wanted to learn how to live a life for Christ as regular people. As attorneys, doctors, insurance agents, construction workers, business owners, husbands, wives, fathers and mothers. Franciscan showed us how to be the light in a black-and-white stigma; you are either religious or not.

However, God providing a community to help support me and encourage me to be better was only half of the story to redemption. I met Kelli hours after stepping on campus for the first time. From the moment I set eyes on her, I started praying for God to give me a chance. Now, let the story be clear: Kelli was way out of my league. She was smart, beautiful, and had a heart of gold. My life at that time was not exactly in order. I was just trying to put all the broken pieces back together. So, for those of you out there who do not believe in miracles, I am here to tell you that they do happen. We hit it off right away, we would spend hours walking around campus getting to know each other. For the first time in a long time, I felt like I was home. But as we continued to spend time together, our relationship eventually reached a point where I knew I had to tell her of my past. I had fallen in love with her, and I needed to let her know why I was really at Franciscan. My confession came as a surprise, and she ended the conversation with, "I need some time to pray about this." There you have it: I was doomed. I spent the next few days praying for a miracle. Sure enough, miracle number two. God had opened her heart to give me a chance. More importantly, He gave her the wisdom and compassion to help me along my journey. Kelli became my rock. She built me up every day, making me feel worthy of her and God's love. It was far from easy, but with God and Kelli at my side, we instilled disciplines and practices that protected our relationship. We waited until we were married before we had sex so we could fulfill the Sacrament of Marriage properly. Which was arguably the hardest accomplishment of my life. The sacrifices we made serve as a living testimony to the graces that followed. Today we celebrate our ninth year of marriage with five beautiful children and more love than one can imagine. My life is truly a blessing, and I give all thanks and glory to God.

"Not all of us can become rich, wise, famous... yet, all of us- yes, all of us- are called to be saints."

-Saint Josemaria Escriva

Anna Carmody

There are only two words to sum up what I believe: *Jesus Christ.*

I was born into a 'normal' Catholic family in Allen Park, Michigan, with an older sister and two younger brothers, all two years apart. My dad had a normal job in sales. Though he was gone a lot, we got used to it. A few years later, my parents felt like God wanted us to home school, an idea which had never before crossed their minds. We followed this calling and home schooled for four years. These years were so fruitful, and we all really grew in our relationship with God during this time.

One day, my mom went on a walk and felt the Lord calling us to be missionaries like John the Baptist and the apostles. Being young, I don't really remember much more than standing up to talk after some Masses, being embarrassed, and being asked the same questions over and over regarding this decision. I had to say goodbye to many people, but I do not think I truly understood how hard that goodbye would be. The goodbye to my grandparents was the one that hit me the hardest. We were really leaving. We sold everything, which was a lot of stuff, and we went to an organization called Family Missions Company (FMC) in Louisiana. We completed our Intake, a three-month-long training program, and I got to experience a new way of living my faith. My faith was not something that had been super strong prior to this experience.

After intake, we were sent to Peru, which quickly became my home. We arrived at the beginning of 2015 and did not leave until the end of 2018. Our first year in Peru was a bit of a blur as we spent our time getting to know the community in our small town of 3,000 people. Our first instinct upon arrival was to try to alleviate everyone's physical suffering, but we quickly learned that the physical suffering in the world is endless and hard to change. I began forming relationships with these people who had nothing but who still laughed and loved and were happy. We then started doing praise and worship, games, and bible studies at the local chapels. Even though these things were so good, we began stretching ourselves too thin. We began staying in our ministry town more, and my sister and I were invited to join our town's cultural dance group of about 50 kids. My sister and I began to make really good friends and shared our faith with them in everything we went through together. We danced, cried, partied, laughed, and learned together. During this time, though, my family was falling apart. We were all going different places and doing different things. We lost all connection. I had memories of a lifetime, but I also hurt more than ever. Though things were really tough, I was able to understand my friends' pain more, and together we fell on Jesus. We started putting on Holy Hours, which is when the Holy Eucharist/Jesus is exposed from the tabernacle. These hours were incredible, as many of our friends had never even been to church before and knew very little about God, yet with tearful eyes they recognized Jesus' presence in the Eucharist.

In our time in Peru, I learned to serve others so relentlessly, which helped me to forget myself, which was good but also bad. I became very humble, a humility I still try to find in a healthy way again, but at the same time I lost myself, not doing the things I enjoy doing. Then, a missionary on a short-term mission trip felt God wanted him to give me a book about Mother Teresa, called *Come Be My Light*. I historically haven't read much, but I accepted it and was pretty desperate for a change with God. Admittedly, it took me a year and a half to start reading it, but once I did I had the realization that Mother Teresa MADE IT TO HEAVEN!!! My soul was in pain, and the sound of Heaven was sweet. I had never thought much about the saints before that.

Shortly after that mission trip, we left Peru. My heart broke into many pieces, and I was tired. I really left my life behind that time. When we had left Michigan, I was so young, but leaving Peru was very different. We came back to the States for a year: 3 months of resting, 1 month of vacation, 3 months of praying and discerning, 4 months of fundraising, and 1 month of getting ready to go to our next missionary post... Kenya, Africa. During that year in the States, I had few friends and moved a lot. It made me ask myself if God is enough.

We arrived in Kenya in 2019. The four of us kids started school, which was crazy! White people aren't really accepted here and are treated very differently. I made some friends and eventually had a good time in school, but the fact that the school days are 11 hours was just too much. It drained me of all energy, and my prayer time was terrible. The church here is pretty developed, and they are not in as desperate need of missionaries as some other places are. We brought that to prayer and have discerned that God wants us to go to Puerto Rico next. I'm alone a lot of the time, and not just because of quarantine. It's a hard life, but it's worth it a million times over. I wrote this in pencil first to symbolize that I am a pencil in God's hands, as Mother Teresa said. Also, I can do all things through Him who strengthens me. Since I believe that strongly, I think we can all be saints. I don't even know where that quote is from in the Bible, because even though I'm a missionary, I'm also a normal person! It sounded a little far-fetched for me the first time that I thought "I can be a saint," or "I could go to Heaven." But I truly believe it, and the way to achieve it is to just live for God today.

"God sends us friends to be our firm support in the whirlpool of struggle. In the company of friends we will find strength to attain our sublime ideal."

-Saint Maximilian Kolbe

Justin Edin

"Rejoice always, pray without ceasing, give thanks in all circumstances; for this is the will of God in Christ Jesus for you."

-1 Thessalonians 5:16-18

On April 26, 2019, my wife and I found out that our son Jasper had Spina Bifida. Spina Bifida is a neural tube defect, a type of birth defect of the brain, spine, or spinal cord. It happens if the spinal column of the fetus doesn't close completely during the first month of pregnancy. The spinal cord is then left exposed to the amniotic fluid, which is toxic to it and damages the spinal cord more and more over time. The higher the opening in the spine, the higher in the body the nerve damage can be. Jasper's opening was in the middle of his lumbar area. When I found out, I was immediately shocked and, quickly after, sad and angry. All I could ask God was, "Why?"

Thankfully for my family, God had blessed us with my wife and our children's mother, Tamber. She prayerfully led me back to God, and we prayed for healing for our son and strength. We soon learned that we might qualify for an in-utero surgery to seal the opening in Jasper's back, which could potentially mitigate the amount of damage that would be done to his nervous system than if we carried him to term with no intervention. We returned to our home and prayerfully came to the decision that we would have the surgery. We wanted to make sure we chose that path not out of fear or mistrust but out of faith and hope.

The next couple of weeks were very stressful as we waited for test results, did consults, and met with the doctors on our team. Since Tamber needed to be close to the special hospital that would do the in-utero surgery and delivery, in case any problems arose, we needed to be prepared to move her to the cities for the duration of the surgery, pregnancy, birth and following NICU stay. Throughout those weeks, I don't know how to really describe it, but I felt more at peace than I thought I should have. In returning to work, once we had hit the waiting-to-find-out stage, many of my co-workers let me know that they had been praying for us. We also started getting messages from extended family and friends who were praying and enlisting people they knew to pray. I told Tamber that I knew others MUST be praying because I could feel it lifting me up when I was weary or wanted to despair. The green light for the surgery finally came on May 9th, and God came through for us with places to stay via my sister-in-law and a great-aunt who both lived in the cities, who took us in and loved us through that trying time. He even sent one of our local deacons to pray over us and to bless us with holy water from Fatima in the middle of a Dairy Queen parking lot as we left town.

On May 17th, Tamber and Jasper had the surgery to seal the opening in his back. We felt such joy and peace settle over us that morning, and afterward the doctor was very excited about how smoothly the surgery and repair went. After a summer with many blessings and trials, Jasper was born by planned c-section on August 8th at 36 weeks. He was perfect. The scar on his back had healed so well that he could lay on his back within the first few days. We came to find out over time that, as a result of the blessing of this surgery and countless prayers, his Spina Bifida was presenting in a much less severe way and he had much better nerve function than expected for the height of his spinal opening. However, while some of the Spina Bifida issues were resolving and hopes of returning home soon were high, we were thrown the curveball of discovering that Jasper was missing several ribs on his left side, which was complicating his ability to breathe properly. God helped us deal with our disappointment and to weather the two-month stay at Children's Hospital until Jasper was strong enough and the doctors were confident we could care for him safely at home, with  continuous oxygen and a gastrostomy tube to feed him. During that time, He surrounded us with love from family, friends, and strangers, many of whom we met during our stay at the hospital and one of whom gifted us a small vial of holy water from Lourdes to bless

Jasper with. We are happy to say he is now one year old, and while he still needs some oxygen support and tube feedings, he is growing in ability and strength every day. His future ability to walk is yet unknown, but he has the loving light of God in his eyes and his sweet, silly grin. We look forward to continuing to see how God uses this joyful little soul He has blessed us with.

The road has not been easy. Without God and the power of our faithful family, friends, and neighbors, I am not sure where we would be. While Jasper will bear burdens and continue to face challenges ahead, I believe that God's plan and will for him is perfect. I also believe that God never gives us more than we can handle and that what He challenges us with is meant to bring our souls closer to Him and to His Kingdom. Through this experience, I have learned on a deeper level what the power of prayer truly is. I am thankful for those prayers, and I am grateful to walk alongside Jesus my Savior through these trials, experiencing the love and generosity that fills our lives.

I will end with strongly recommending adding the rosary to your prayer life. The intercession of Mary has been truly powerful in my life, and I credit her for helping me many times beyond what I could ever deserve. God bless you and keep you, and may his angels watch over you all the days of your life.

Victoria Hammond

"Consider it all joy, my brothers, when you encounter various trials, for you know that the testing of your faith produces perseverance."

-James 1:2-3

Belief can be a struggle. And that struggle can be a beautiful gift. Since I was quite young, I've had struggles with finding peace in belief. Fear of hell was a very real thing to young Catholic-since-the-cradle me. And I desperately didn't want to "not be good enough" and spend eternity in punishment. Looking back, it's kind of humorous that this sweet, innocent, very-much-trying-to-do-the-right-thing little girl had these very intense fears of something that I now know the Good Father never would have let happen to her. I wasn't going to "accidentally" go to hell. But I did have those fears, and I carried them with me into college. So the good, Mass-going (sometimes even weekday-Mass-going), sacrament-receiving young woman still struggled.

And sometimes the struggle was downright frightening. On occasions, I would experience this event (for lack of a better word) where nothing felt real. It usually happened late at night, when I was alone and everyone else was sleeping. I just felt unreal. I would describe it as emptiness or darkness, but that feels like it's underselling it. In these spirals, I would have thoughts such as, time isn't real, and people may not even be real. What's eternity? What purpose does anything have? Why am I alive? My body would sometimes shake with just the overwhelming-ness of it. There were many tears. Often I would eventually fall asleep. Or I would eventually get out of the spiral, but if it was particularly bad, I would just feel so fragile and tender the day after, that "made of glass" feeling. I tried not to think too hard about anything because there was a real possibility I could spiral again.

And yet, I still went to church, still prayed twice a day every day, and I still chose belief. Even when I started having doubts and just felt like this whole Catholic Faith thing was really hard, I chose to keep doing it. After college graduation and working my dream job, I just felt kind of empty in regards to faith. In hindsight, I think the beautiful structure of the Catholic Faith is one thing that kept me going. Another was the strong fight of Jesus for me. Because when I let myself really consider the possibility that the Faith wasn't true, I knew it was true. I *knew* it was true. So I chose again. One more day, one more moment, I chose.

But, as you can imagine, this struggle certainly didn't feel comfortably sustainable. At all. So, God intervened. He sent someone who knew Him better than me, and she sent a simple private Facebook message, asking if I'd want to join a group from the area on a mission trip to Peru. And before I even thought about it, I felt the 'Yes.' I am NOT a traveler. I had NO aspirations of traveling around the world, and yet, this 'yes' was so filled with peace and so sure. So, I went.

On this mission trip were some of the most amazingly holiness-striving people I have ever met. Some of them had these awesome, miracle-filled testimonies. And I just… didn't. After hearing the testimony of one of the full-time missionaries, we had some prayer time to pray on and think about our own testimony story. I can still picture that little chapel in Peru, me sitting on the wooden pew with no cushion, in the non-air conditioned, yet peaceful and simple place, and I can still hear my sniffles as I wondered, "Do I really know Jesus?" I felt like I did not have this deep friendship with Him like I saw others have. Then, internally I heard, "You know we're friends." So, being the logical person I am, I sat there and compared my relationship to Him to my relationship with my best friend from college. I turn to her and talk to her about things all of the time… and I did that with Jesus, too. During those 3 a.m. freak-outs, I'd pray. When I was excited about something, I'd say a "thank-you" prayer. Just randomly throughout the day, I'd pray. I'd talk with Him, and He was always there. He was my constant, THE most loyal presence in my life. I realized that He listens, attentively and fully. He doesn't "get bored" with what I'm saying and interrupt or walk away. He truly understands. I found I DO have friendship with Him. While this friendship may not include a 2-hour-long adoration while speaking in tongues, or having many large miracles occur around me, it does include reaching out in prayer when something exciting, or scary, or really anything happens. That's how I do friendship. My favorite kind of friendship is made up of the everyday things, doing life together, and being a constant support in someone's life; and Jesus knows that and thinks it's beautiful because God designed me this way. This big "reversion" (conversion, but having never really left the Faith) moment in my life was basically just realizing that God loves me and desires friendship in the ways in which I feel most loved. There was no huge physical miracle, no fire and lights, just a beautifully sweet revelation in a humble Peruvian chapel.

So, life continued on. Suddenly, I started seeing God more in the little things. I might have three songs in a row on the radio that I really love that help lift me up: mini miracle. Friends making a visit right when I feel like my faith is starting to slip and encouraging me again: mini miracle. My godson wanting to read "godmother stories" with me, getting that random prize I wanted in my mobile game, finding a parking space on the right level when I'm running late, a particular homily that feels like it was spoken just to me: all mini miracles. God shows up. Not just in fire, flashing lights, deep voices, miraculous healings, rumblings, and earthquakes (and *thank goodness!* because that is so not the way I desire to be loved), but He loves me with constancy and loyalty, knows the true me, and shows His love in beautiful, quirky little ways. God knows that this is how I desire to be loved, and He is the best at it because He made me. Therefore, He also thinks it's a beautiful way to love: choosing little, constant, amazingly humbling ways to love me every day.

As far as some of the ways of reciprocating that love, I still purposely pray twice a day. But don't be fooled into thinking it's some big, miraculous, so-holier-than-thou-on-my-knees-that-you-will-never-be-able-to-do-it thing. It's when I wake up and before I go to sleep, because that's when I remember to do it. And sometimes the morning is really rushed because I hit snooze more times than I had time for. And sometimes the evening is a bit half-hearted because I DEFINITELY should have been going to bed a long time before I did. However, I choose to do it. Just like I choose to go to Mass, pray throughout the day, serve where I can both in the church and at my job, and learn more about the Faith, I do it because I choose friendship. I choose love.

In the interest of total honesty, I do have to say: I still struggle. I still struggle HARD sometimes. I still sometimes experience those events with feelings of emptiness and darkness, but now I choose to offer them up. I have found that when I make the choice to offer it up, the struggle is often easier to deal with. Sometimes "easier" means it ends quicker, I don't spiral as far, or I can exit the feelings of empty and nothingness. But sometimes easier means that I'm given the consolation that this suffering has meaning. Jesus made the ultimate offering for us: He suffered body and soul for our redemption. And He invites us to take part in His plan for redemption. Perhaps the call to be part of His redemption is to work large, physical, miraculous deeds. Perhaps the call is to preach to large crowds or to inspire through huge conferences. Perhaps the call is to love the way I most desire to love and be loved. Perhaps my call is to offer up sufferings for those I love, those I don't love as I should, and those I don't or barely know throughout my everyday life, as a constant, loyal way to love. I can offer up so many things, like struggles with belief, my hunger as I wait to take my break at work, my frustration with a family member, my anxieties of *still* being single, or the miles on my jog. In choosing to offer these things up, I'm loving God and my neighbor. I'm allowing God to use these things for more good than I could ever accomplish on my own. God can do all things, and I think the miracle He does in my life is blessing me with the gift of these "little" sufferings to give me a part in the saving of souls.

Belief can be a struggle. That struggle can be a gift. Those ample opportunities to choose love, and therefore to love God, are His miracles for me. And I am *incredibly* thankful for these ready-made opportunities to love!

"Above all, trust in the slow work of God."

-Pierre Teilhard de Chardin, S.J.

Jared Beumer

"Although the temptations are strong, a whole wave of doubts beats against my soul, and discouragement stands by, ready to enter into the act. The Lord, however, strengthens my will, against which all the attempts of the enemy are shattered as if against a rock. I see how many actual graces God grants me; these support me ceaselessly. I am very weak, and I attribute everything solely to the grace of God."

-Diary of Saint Maria Faustina Kowalska, 1086 (page 406)

I was raised in a very Catholic family. In elementary school, every day before I would get dropped off, I would go to daily Mass with my parents. It didn't take long before everyone knew, and I was voted 'most religious' in the grade for our yearbook multiple years in a row. Every year, with a sense of pride, I was so happy that all of my hard effort was being recognized. But in reality, no matter how hard I tried I couldn't get out of my parents' devotion, so I was more or less dragged along. I continued to go to Catholic school throughout middle and high school, this time being able to go to Mass only on the days necessary for the Catholic Faith. I knew more Bible trivia and facts about the life of Jesus than the majority of the other students, and I believed I was a good Catholic because of my weekly Mass attendance, my knowledge about Jesus, and the fact that I went to confession every 6 months.

I didn't realize until my freshman year of college that while I was doing everything that I thought made me a good practicing Catholic, I was missing one huge element: I had never taken hold of my own faith. After being raised Catholic and understanding what my parents had said about the Faith, I was only following along with the Faith because I liked what it was teaching and it was what I was brought up to believe. Somehow, while sitting in my dorm room one day, I had a stark realization that being Catholic was more than what I was doing, and that if I really believed what I was brought up to believe, I needed to make some changes. The first was that I needed to take control of my own faith. I could no longer ride on the coat-tails of my parents' faith and just go through the motions, going to church only when I knew they would require. If this was going to be my faith and ultimately play such a crucial role in eternity, I needed to take it more seriously and actually live my faith, rather than just showing up to Mass on Sundays. I knew exactly what this meant, too. I knew there was much work that needed to be done, but like a giant boulder sitting between me and the road ahead, there was only one thing I could see: my addiction to porn.

I do not know exactly at what age I was first introduced to porn; I believe it was right between elementary school and middle school.

Without a proper understanding of what I was really seeing and doing, I with stupid excitement dove deeper into sin with neither the intention of turning back or stopping. By the time I realized what I was really doing, a few years had passed and now I couldn't stop. I couldn't remember the last time I had heard a homily about it in church and there was no way I was going to ask for further information. I thought that since the Church doesn't talk about it much, it must not affect a lot of people. I had gotten myself into this problem, and since I must be the only one here, it was up to me to get out by myself if I was going to save face and hide what I was doing.

And that was me, sitting at about 14 years old, already a few years in and now facing the realization of what I had gotten myself into. I was so embarrassed and ashamed because what I was doing was so far from what my parents had taught me. I was waiting for the answer on what to do, but with so much shame I couldn't ask for help. It was a shame that made me feel like the only one in the world going through this, a shame that destroyed my will and separated me further from God. I think everyone has a desire to show the best parts of who they are and subtly hide what they don't like about themselves. However, the aspects that we often want to hide the most can have the biggest impact on our interactions. For me, the person I found myself to be was at odds with the person I was raised to be, so not only did I find myself separated from God, but I was also unable to have meaningful relationships with people my own age. From a young age I had been taught to be a good and holy person, so if I didn't see myself as anything but a fraud and an outsider, how could I expect anyone else to see me in a different light? I was afraid that people would see what I really did and would want nothing to do with me. I thought they would see who I was, and that terrified me. I allowed this addiction in my life to rob me of everything I wanted: to feel loved by God and to have friends. But at the time I didn't realize that it was the sin that robbed me of those things; I thought it was just me.

Obviously, trying to fix the problem on my own went about as well as one could expect: I continued to struggle throughout the remainder of high school, and I dragged the problem that I thought I would outgrow or overcome into college with me. Knowing that something now needed to be done about it, I had no idea what to do, so I decided to go to confession. Being honest with the priest for probably the first time ever, I felt like I was telling the priest something he had never heard before. Fortunately, priests have heard a thing or two, and instead of getting yelled at, he actually smiled at me and said that I had made a good confession. However, I still felt like I was all alone, because in my mind no good Catholic would ever do what I was doing, and I felt like a fraud sitting in a pew next to others vastly holier than me. I had felt separated from the rest of congregation like this for many years, but it felt like it was getting worse. This feeling I could not escape lead to another problem: the belief that no matter how many times I went to confession, I could still never become who God wanted me to be, so in His eyes I was a failure.

After feeling like I would never measure up to Gods standards or desires for me, I began to feel like all of the stories I had heard about God loving the worst sinners and that every sin is forgivable somehow only counted for everyone else but me. Time after time I had fallen into sin, and no matter how many times I went to confession the same thing happened. I still went to confession as much as I could, but I felt incomplete and separated from Gods love. It was such a hard place to be, feeling such a desire to overcome my faults and wanting to be loved but feeling like I was just out of reach of God's love. This feeling was so commonplace for so long that it somehow had become a truth that I held in my heart, and no matter what I did I couldn't overcome this feeling.

Even once I overcame this addiction, I still felt this disconnect with God. I felt like a fence post sitting alone on a hill; every time I sinned, no matter the sin, there would be a nail that was driven into me, and I would slowly accumulate more and more nails until I went to confession where they were all taken out. Then I would be once again sin-free without a nail in me, but still sitting alone on a hill, this time with all the holes that were left behind from the nails. I felt so broken. As the years passed and I graduated college, I slowly started gaining a stronger relationship with God despite my disbelief in reciprocated love. I believed my relationship with God was amazing and couldn't get any better. I would still go to weekly confession, because once I was able to remove the boulder from my path, I was able to see how many other obstacles were really in the way of me being the man God wanted me to be.

Last year, I was able to go on a Steubenville retreat as a chaperone, and that forever changed my relationship with God. At the time I had been married for just under three years, with two kids. My wife said it was always her dream to have a husband who had gone on a TEC or Steubenville retreat, and because I had not been on either one yet, she was really pressuring me to go. I won't lie, I went somewhat reluctantly, because my son was having many health complications and he had multiple surgeries that still left many unanswered questions that could have serious repercussions. We almost lost him after a surgery on his kidney had failed, so leaving was the last thing on my mind. My wife, however, convinced me to go, and the thought of getting a good night of sleep, some rosaries in, and my first uninterrupted Mass in years sounded very enticing at the same time. I was having fun helping the youth and had a tiny hope that I would be able to have a powerful experience, even though the trip was not intended for me. I had completely forgotten about how I now had a broken belief of unreciprocated love with God. I don't know how many of you have been on a Steubenville retreat or a similar retreat, but one of the events for the weekend was adoration with everyone in one large group. I had been to adoration many times before, but this was unlike anything I have ever experienced and is the closest to what I imagine Heaven will be like. It was completely unworldly. As adoration started and I was praying and watching the way the Holy Spirit was working in this huge gymnasium, I couldn't help but be astounded at the impact that it was having on so many people. The priest brought the monstrance all the way around the room and then turned it directly at me, as if it was meant just for me, and I heard the voice of Jesus whispering in my soul, answering the one question in my life I didn't know I needed answered. With one sentence, He fixed my broken perception of Him and overcame all my questions about His love for me. He said, "It is not about what you've done or who you are; you are a child of God and God loves His children because that is who He is." My heart was mended in an instant, and all the years of feeling unloved by the Creator of the universe were washed away. Words cannot describe the love that God has for us, and now out of all of the uncertainties in my life, the one thing that I will never forget is that my God loves me more than I could ever imagine, even when I fail.

My belief that I could never be who God wanted me to be, after living what felt like my whole life in sin, left me feeling at times like there was no point and that the fight was not worth fighting because the outcome would always be the same. I couldn't have been further from the truth. What to me looked like a never-ending problem that was untamable, was really a call for me from God to never give up. It is a good thing that God has a lot of patience, because I needed it. Day after day, week after week, I could never see the difference, but looking back now, the true blessing I received from God was that no matter how many times I fell, God would bend down and pick me up as many times as I would ask. See, God never asked for perfection from us; it is what He desires for us all, but the only thing He requires of us is to try. If we stop carrying our crosses we will start finding ourselves farther and farther from Jesus, not because He is walking away, but because we are refusing to walk towards Him.

"See what love the Father has lavished on us, that we should be called children of God! And that is what we are! The reason the world does not know us is that it did not know him."
- 1 John 3:1

Ann Marschel

"For where your treasure is, there also will your heart be."

-Matthew 6:21

As I stood in the shower weeping, I realized how broken I was. Depleted physically, drained emotionally, and spiritually imbalanced, I knew I could handle no more. The only way out would be if I surrendered. Surrendered once again. Surrendered my plans, my way, and my concerns. Turning my worry and desire for control over to the Lord. And I did just that. I prayed. It was an ugly prayer, but an honest one. Tears streamed down my face and my lower lip quivered as I prayed. I told God I couldn't do this anymore. I wanted them all to be healthy again. I wanted things to go back to how they used to be. Finally, I shared with God what He knew all along: I shared myself. After I was done spilling my heart, I listened. There was no loud voice or lightning strike. None at all. Instead, I was reminded of a book I had read called *Everyday Sacrament: The Messy Grace of Parenting,* by Laura Fanucci. One of her chapters spoke about how after taking a shower as a new mother she was refreshed, renewed, and restored. She related this ordinary, everyday occurrence of taking a shower back to the sacrament of Baptism.

As the water washed over me, a quiet stirring in my heart told me that everything would be okay. I did not have to be strong every moment of every day. It was okay for me to let my guard down. It was okay to be worn out. Most importantly, it was okay for me to hand over the messiness of life and ask for help. He was there and He loved me in spite of it all. All I needed to do was rely on Him, to allow Him to be my comfort and strength. To realize that He was in control and He would take care of me and everyone I loved. To realize that He had never left my side and wanted me to fall into His protective and loving arms.

I stayed in that hot, steamy shower, sobbing longer, but with a strength and peace that I had not had before entering it. The Lord was there with me, like always. All I needed to do was let Him in and ask Him to help me.

The next few days were tough. In God's infinite mercy, He allowed certain people to reach out to me. He gave me small, quiet opportunities to surrender everything to Him and He allowed wisdom and clarity to come from the bleak situation I was facing. More so, He showed me how to let go and let Him take the wheel: the wheel that I had been trying to hold on to and steer for so long by myself.

My name is Ann and this is my conversion story. It is not one that is dramatic and worthy of a Grammy award. Rather, it is one that is simple and constant. My conversion did not happen in one moment, but has happened in a series of well-orchestrated events that only He could have foreseen. Events that, as I look back, have allowed me to love Him and the Catholic faith more each and every day. So, with that, let us begin...

I've always been a learner. Going to school was fun for me and learning new things has always fascinated me. This is true not only in my professional life as a Natural Family Planning Instructor, licensed teacher, and healthy relationships speaker, but also in my spiritual life.

I'm always learning, always growing in my spiritual life, and with that the Lord is always tapping at my heart and helping me become the best-version-of-myself. He wants me to get to Heaven to be with Him, just like He wishes for all of His children. He sometimes shows me His plans and other times He is in the background. He's my friend and is trying to kindle in me a fire of His love and a faith that is deep. I've learned that He has never left me even in those deep, dark moments. No; instead, it was I who abandoned Him.

Through my years, I've learned that all I need to do is respond to His promptings and invitations to seek Him and His kingdom. This happens during those quiet moments I'm given throughout the day. When I have that inkling that I should smile at a stranger or extend a listening ear to that person who feels alone even though I'm in a hurry. When I feel it on my heart to pray for others or love that person who is the hardest to love. Or, most importantly, when I have been hurt by someone and need to forgive them even though I want to hold a grudge and blame them for all the pain I'm experiencing. When I have responded by listening and attuning to the Holy Spirit's gentle nudges in these moments, I have seen God work miracles. I have learned that He will take care of me and all of His children.

My first conversion, I do not remember. All I have are pictures of that conversion and stories from the people who were there. That first conversion was when I was welcomed into the Catholic Church: my Baptism. It was then that I was given the grace to begin my relationship with the Lord. Yes, I was a baby, but this allowed my soul to start on the path to sainthood.

As I grew, I had other moments of conversion. I received my First Confession and my First Communion, and I was in a family that encouraged honesty, faith, hope, and love. I was learning more about my Faith, receiving more grace from God, and in turn discovering that there was more to God and Faith than just what I was hearing from those around me. I would say the first time I remember feeling the Lord's presence would have been in middle school when I went on a Steubenville Trip with a girl who I didn't know that well. Little did I know that this girl would be my best friend for life.

It all started when her mom approached my mom asking if I would be interested in going on a Catholic youth conference with her daughter. I was up for trying new things and my parents supported me, so off I went. We traveled to Franciscan University that summer. The one detail I can remember from that trip was the procession of the Monstrance in Eucharistic Adoration. I can remember hundreds of us sweaty teenagers kneeling on matted grass under a large tent. My attempt to look good for the boys that surrounded my hormone-raging self was not working, since sweat dripped down my forehead and my hair was frizzier than frayed carpet. But as the priest carried the shiny Monstrance throughout the tightly-lined rows, none of that mattered. Instead, I was entranced by the large breeze that blew through the tent as Jesus passed me. It made me pause. At that moment I couldn't describe what happened or why my life was changed, but I had a strong sense of peace and knowledge that this whole "God being present in the Eucharist" was not something that was made up.

The next time I had a conversion, it happened unexpectedly. Since I was a young girl, I wanted to have a sister. I had two younger brothers, but I wanted the sister connection that I always saw portrayed on television. As I grew and the years passed, even with many prayers and hints to my parents, I had given up on the notion that I would have a sister. Then one day, to my excitement, my parents announced at the dinner table that they were going to have another baby. I was fourteen at the time, and I soon found out that our family would be welcoming a baby girl. I remember tears of joy flowing down my face. As I watched my mother's womb grow, my heart swelled with the thought that God did love and care about me. Then, after a long time of anticipation, my beautiful sister was born. She was a true delight and gift to us all and still is today. When I think of her or see her, I'm reminded that the Lord hears our prayers always. He may not answer them in our timing or in the way we might expect, but He knows us, hears us, and wants us to be joyful.

After high school, I went off to college. I ended up attending a secular college and was excited for the possibility to spread my wings and help others "see" the light of Christ. As hopeful as I was to help "convert" others, I experienced great difficulty in doing just that. I found myself surrounded by people who were okay with things that I did not agree with, people who were living a life that I did not want to live. I soon found myself in an environment that was morally corrupt, and I was lonely and started questioning many things. My prayer life was at its all-time lowest and I found it hard to be the only one not going to the parties, drinking, and engaging in the "hook-up" culture. Thankfully, I had a wonderful spiritual director and went home on the weekends for Sunday Mass. If I did not attend weekly Mass and have my faith-filled spiritual director to help me navigate that bumpy road that year, I know I would be a different person today. At this point, I seemed to be going through the motions more than fully embracing the life Christ was calling me to.

In the spring semester of my freshman year, I ended up traveling with two vibrant priests (one of whom was my spiritual director) and another gal from my parish to Nashville, TN. We went to visit the

Motherhouse of the Nashville Dominican Sisters. These sisters had an unspeakable joy about them. Their faith radiated through their smiles and the simple task of eating a meal in silence felt like I was partaking in adoration. Being with these sisters who had Jesus as their best friend, while partaking in their devout and loving prayer life, brought me back to the faith I once knew and had before it became buried my first year in college. These sisters were filled to the brim with Christ's light. Their apostolate was teaching, which was where my heart was. After leaving their Motherhouse, I soon found myself wondering if I was called to become a religious sister. Once I returned home, I found a renewed sense of vigor in my spiritual life and attended Mass and adoration frequently. Many older people within my parish started asking if I was going to become a nun. I had been discerning for years and wondered if God was calling me to become a sister, but for some reason when thinking about entering a convent, my heart was not as peace. I found that discerning my Vocation was extremely difficult.

Since middle school, I had been praying about my Vocation. At one point during this time of discernment, a random woman came up to me at a Catholic bookstore. She showed me a prayer card of St. Anne and started reciting this prayer, "Dear St. Ann, find me a man as fast as you can." She said she had prayed this prayer and soon found her spouse. Knowing that the Holy Spirit can work in many ways, I soon started praying this prayer, still not knowing where God was leading me. I wanted to know what Vocation the Lord was calling me to immediately, but He made me wait. I am not good at waiting. I like to get things done, but through this struggle of waiting I had to trust God and rely on Him. I had to believe that He would show me my path.

Returning the next year to the same college, I was on a new adventure, studying abroad in a castle with 32 other students in Alnwick, England. I was excited but didn't know a single person that was going with me. I like adventure and meeting new people, so that didn't bother me. The one thing I questioned was how I was going to get to Mass every Sunday. The amazing thing about the Catholic Faith is that no matter where you are in the world, the flow and parts of the

Mass are the same, so even if the language is different you can still participate in and pray the Mass. I soon found a parish community that was a couple blocks away from the castle, as well as a convent that was right across the road from the castle too! You cannot tell me that wasn't divine intervention. ☺ Being all the way across the ocean and choosing to go to Mass when I could have just stayed in bed allowed me to grow in my faith and challenged me to make it a priority in my life. My relationship with Christ blossomed, and I knew I wanted to continue being Catholic.

Studying abroad helped me grow in many ways, but I was still left with uncertainty about my future Vocation. I had always loved children and was drawn to the idea of married life, but I had not found the right man yet. Now that I look back, I see how God protected my heart many times since He knew once I fell in love with the man I would marry and that love was reciprocated, I would be hooked for life.

Once I returned home, my heart was still uneasy in where God wanted me. I was stronger in my faith, but not necessarily in trusting what God had in store for me. He then allowed a wonderful, faith-filled, Catholic man to reenter my life. This man pushed me to be a better Catholic Christian, woman, teacher, friend, and sister. He helped bring out the best-version-of-me and continues to do so to this day. As we courted, our faith in God grew and we supported and helped each other. We started as friends, and to this day he is the person I share everything with. We attended Mass together, laughed together, prayed together, worked together, did our Consecration to Mary together, and played sports together. My heart finally found peace in my discernment process, and my time of waiting (which seemed like forever) came to a close when we celebrated our wedding day.

The next conversion in my life was when I became a mother. Becoming a mother is filled with wonder and excitement, yet at the same time a sense of self-doubt. I had always wanted to be a mom, but would I be a good one? God calmed my fears and anxieties, and

He always allowed me to lean on Him. It was with His strength and grace, as well as the people He had put in my life, that I was able to mother my first sweet baby boy. As my son grew and we added more children to our family, the heaviness of all of the needs and wants were weighing me down, but there was always a warm spot in my heart and a soft peacefulness in my soul. My husband, family, and friends were there to support me, and Mother Mary continued to wrap me in her arms and take my prayers to her son Jesus. I was never alone. Instead, I was given a bountiful amount of people who would love, encourage, and pray for me. Through motherhood I've learned to depend less on myself and more on Him. He sustains me in all I do. He makes me whole. Through all the scrapes, bumps, bruises, tears, laughter, hugs, kisses, discipline, and teaching of the Faith, He has been with us all. I often pray to St. Joseph and Mother Mary for their intercession, since parenting proves to have its ups and down. Having done the Consecration to St. Joseph and the Consecration to Mary, I sense their intercession for our family often.

My biggest conversion thus far has happened within the last couple of years. Things in my life were not how I had planned. I found myself wallowing in self-pity and being restless with my life. It seemed as though I could no longer handle all the needs that surrounded me. I knew I wasn't alone, but somehow, I had myself convinced that I had to take care of things myself. Looking back, these were all lies. In the Bible it states, "We can do all things through Christ who strengthens us," yet I lacked this faith in His Word.

I was busy doing good things. I had left my professional life to stay home with my sons. That was a huge leap of faith for me since I had always thought I'd be teaching in the professional world and could never stay at home. Yet, the Lord provided for me as I journeyed to figure out that my worth was not rooted in my profession. No; my worth, I discovered, was rooted in His love for me.

During this time of staying at home, I felt like I wasn't doing enough so I started volunteering for MANY things. Don't worry, they were good things! I was trying to be Christ to those that I took care of and came in contact with. I was teaching in ways that allowed me to use my gifts and talents to bring people closer to Christ and/or to show people how much Christ loved them. However, I soon was so busy and involved that I lost track of my prayer life. I did not have enough energy to give to those I ministered to, my children, my husband, and my friendships, let alone God. The Vocation I knew God had called me to and the one I had prayed about for such a long time soon felt daunting and overwhelming. I found myself exhausted and soon started to lose hope that the things in my life would be okay. I was dealing with hardship within friendships, family life, and within myself. I found myself in a desert: a place where I felt spiritually dry and not feeling the Lord's presence. This spiritual dryness had occurred other times throughout my life, but this time, for the first time, I was feeling hopeless. I soon dreaded going to Mass and would have rather stayed in bed than get up to deal with my daily life. Then, once I was up, I was unable to be present to those in my life. I was always thinking about the next thing, or 'How I could fix this?', or 'What did I do wrong?'

Then one weekend, our kids were sick, so my husband went to an early Sunday Mass and I went by myself to a later Mass. As I drove to church that morning, I was tired. I had sick kids again and some heavy things on my heart. I felt lost in my Vocation and where the Lord wanted me. I saw hurting hearts in my family. I was experiencing the heartache and pain of having friends suffer from fertility issues. Yet, as I drove to church, my cares seemed to be lifted away as I saw the fresh snow fall to the ground like feathers. I love snow, especially the big flakes that are so delicate that they float elegantly down to the ground. Seeing that type of snow reminded me of confession: after confession, our souls are clean like the new snow. Then, when the snow has been on the ground for some time, it starts to get dirty and hard, just like what happens to our souls when we sin. But once we have a new snowfall, it seems to take away all the dark and dirty snow and the ground is clean once again, exactly like when we receive confession. All those sins, all those icky thoughts and feeling and things we did are wiped clean for a new start. As I quickly walked into church by myself that morning, I knew it was going to be special. Mass was a typical Mass, but the priest (a.k.a. the Holy Spirit) spoke directly to my heart that day. He said we need to have Jesus in every aspect of our life and we need to invite Him into every aspect. I needed to be reminded that I was not alone and that all I had to do was invite Him in. After receiving Jesus in Holy Communion, I was given that sense of vigor again. I was reminded that He was still there even though I had not been "feeling" close to Him or questioned why He was allowing all this pain and restlessness into my heart. As humans we feel a lot of emotions, yet sometimes our emotions get the better of us. I was letting my feelings mask the truth of who God is.

After Mass, as I was looking through the bulletin, I noticed a mom's group that was meeting the next day. I had it on my heart that I needed to get involved with a group of faith-filled women, but I always put it off. I mean, come on, I had my stuff together and I didn't need anyone to help me, support me, or challenge me to become a better Catholic...right? But I felt that tug on my heart and I knew I had to try it. I made a call to the leader that night to get more details. She was happy to answer questions and invited me to come the next day and said there was child care available. I was excited, but little did I know that this group of women would become the ones who would uphold me in the struggles and joys that laid ahead.

The next morning, as I met that group of women for the first time, I was amazed. These women were honest, vulnerable, and just like me —broken, yet working to become saints. I had never met women who bared their souls to a complete stranger. I had always felt that I needed to be guarded and protected from other women, since I had been hurt by friends in the past. They challenged me to be me, for me to be honest and to do some soul searching. They allowed me to dig deep and peel back the layers of myself that I was hiding. To reveal the walls I was putting up between myself and God.

Each time we met for our bible study, I realized that I was no longer trusting God that things would be okay. Instead, I was trying to run away from Him and from the hurt I was experiencing inside. I honestly would have rather become a hermit at this point in my life instead of acknowledging the woundedness I needed to work on. I didn't want my pride to be exposed. I didn't want to let anyone know that I felt like a hypocrite. I didn't want to feel those hard feelings and work on healing my brokenness. I didn't want to show anyone, not even myself, how much I had been hurting from past and current experiences. But it was through peeling back these layers of myself, going through different studies (*Wild Goose* and *Fearless and Free*), and being with these women that I was able to acknowledge my brokenness and rejoice in my goodness. This group of women supported me through this journey, called me out when I was prideful, and helped me navigate my journey.

We all have choices in our lives that need to be made. I've learned that I cannot live in the past and hold on to guilt or resentment. This is not healthy. I can only control how I respond to situations. I'm still working on this, and each day I try to surrender and give it to God. Reading and praying with His Word, as well as spending time with Him in prayer, has enabled me to do this more easily. Overall, I learned that if I did not go through some struggles in my life, I would not have been able to acknowledge how much I need God in my life. I can put my trust in myself, my husband, family, and friends, but ultimately, I will be let down. God is in control and we can trust Him.

My conversion continues every time I take a step outside and view nature. This is God's own painting for me. Every time I look into the brown eyes of my boys, I'm reminded that God chose me to be their mother and I am good enough to do the job He has entrusted me to do. At night, when I crawl into bed next to my husband and hold his hand as we drift off to sleep, I'm reminded of how faithful God is to me. He has allowed me to fulfill my Vocation through the Sacrament of Matrimony to my best friend. As I work in various teaching positions, I am satisfied because God has given me the talents and gifts I need to do those jobs. He has led me to these positions and wants to use me to help others.

Through all of these small conversions, I am still broken. I still work every day, and sometimes every minute, on becoming a better-version-of-myself. There are times of joy and happiness on this journey, and there are times of feeling battered and bruised. I've learned that it's how I choose to handle these moments that make me who I am.

God wants all of us to be joyful. He wants the very best for us. All we need to do is invite Him in and listen. He's always there, in every moment. He sometimes presents Himself in the quiet stirrings of our heart, through a friend or neighbor, or even sometimes through the smile of the cashier at the store. We never know when He will present Himself. We just need to be attuned to His Word through Scripture and His promptings within our heart, which is developed through prayer.

So, what's your conversion story? When, where, or who makes you feel closest to God? Those are the things or people you want to keep in your life. I also encourage you to think about those times in your life when you have felt the furthest from God. Maybe you still do? I would challenge you to ask yourself, are you the one who is pushing Him away - putting up walls, not receiving the sacraments, not feeling like you are loved enough to be forgiven? If this is you, I'm here to tell you that is not God's voice. I would know, since I've heard these lies. Our Lord would never tell you that you are unlovable. You are not! You are His beloved and He calls you by name. He knows how many strands of hair are on your head. We are all precious to Him, and each day He gives us opportunities for our hearts to be converted back to Him. So the question is, "Will we embrace these moments of grace and mercy or will we turn away from Him?"

"In my deepest wound I saw your glory, and it dazzled me."

-Saint Augustine

Morgan Ness

"After you have suffered for a little while, the God of all grace, who called you to His eternal glory in Christ, will Himself perfect, confirm, strengthen and establish you."

-1 Peter 5:10

Many of those closest to me would describe me as a very "yellow" person. My personality is very bubbly, and I try my best to find the positive out of every situation in life. I take advantage of every situation in which I get to laugh, and I am mainly known to never be serious. I love to dance and sing, even though I should not be allowed to do so in public. For what seemed like an extra-long winter, however, I was anything but that happy-yellow girl I used to know, and I learned what it meant to root your happiness in Jesus.

I grew up attending Mass most Sundays and always knew about God and Jesus. I knew He created the world and all of us, but what I failed to see growing up was the never-ending love He has for His creation. It wasn't until my first year of a Christian summer camp that I felt God's presence and knew what it meant to be on God's team. A good friend of mine had attended Camp Lebanon the year before and invited me to go with her. Little did I know that my life would be forever changed. My eyes were opened to the love of God, and I was overwhelmed with His presence. Everybody at camp had this radiating joy, and for the first time, I felt like I really belonged somewhere. I belong on God's team. The pastor at camp my first year emphasized the importance of living for God's team every day. The verse used to give the description of what it means to be on God's team was Colossians 3:12-14:

Therefore as God's chosen people, holy and dearly loved, clothe yourselves with compassion, kindness, humility, gentleness, and patience. Bear with each other, and forgive one another if any of you has a grievance against someone. Forgive as the Lord forgave you. And over all these virtues, put on love which binds them together in perfect unity.

This verse openly summarizes our job as Christians to love those around us, and was described to me at camp as "putting on your team uniform." As I began my walk with Christ, this verse changed my outlook and impacted the way I want to live every day as a follower of Jesus.

While my relationship with God was strong at camp, I often found it difficult to maintain that relationship back at home. With my religion classes ending after tenth grade and an increase in challenging school work and competitive volleyball, distractions grew. My junior year became the hardest year for me mentally, and I was in a constant battle with my mental health. An inescapable dark storm suddenly consumed my mind. Winter came, and with it an extremely hard war between me and my own thoughts. I was drained, exhausted, and unhappy. School consumed most of my time, and it felt never-ending. I convinced myself the classes were too hard, and that I wasn't smart enough. I felt unmotivated, unworthy, unwanted. I stopped putting on God's team uniform and began to wear my own. Many of my closest friends had begun to walk away from me, and I didn't feel good enough for anyone, not even myself. I failed to see God's bigger plan to fill my life with people who are better for me. Every mistake I made during that time, whether in sports or in relationships, weighed extremely heavily on me. The enemy said, "You have little value here," and I listened. I no longer liked who I was. I felt it was easy for people to leave me, and I convinced myself that many had. I didn't want to let anyone in. I tried so hard to hide my pain, and I smiled through most of it. I feared people would worry about me, and I knew I was loved, but something was missing. I felt as though nobody understood what I was going through. I felt utterly alone. Of course, I knew Jesus was by my side but His presence felt nonexistent because I forgot to pursue Him. And while pursuing God does not grant you endless happiness, it sure does help.

Further into the year, I began to make more time for God. I started a plan to read my Bible every day, and with that, I found my purpose again. I was able to cast my anxieties onto Him, and I learned that some battles are just too hard to walk through alone. I placed it into God's hands, finally understanding that He is greater. My strength is rooted in Him. I was handed a battle I didn't think would end, and His light shone through. I had begun to surround myself with a group of Christian girls who would uplift me and hold me accountable every day. They had been there the whole time, but I failed to notice. His love healed my heart, and my worth was finally found in Him. While

I didn't choose this battle, God knew there was a purpose to my pain. I've been able to grow stronger in my faith. I've found purpose in my life again. My heart is filled with His never-ending joy, and my purpose is to share that joy.

Although not every day may feel joyful, and my battle may be far from over, I know that through Him the battle is already won. It's okay to lose sight of your faith, as long as you regain what you lost. It will only make you stronger in the end. There is purpose in every struggle. I may only be seventeen, but I know that God can and will use my story. Take advantage of every misfortune; you never know just how good it will feel when God uses it for your gain. God never promised us an easy journey. The waves will crash, and our eyes will unfocus from Him. The battle won't be easy, but the battle is His.

"Do not be afraid to be the saints of the new millennium!"

-Saint John Paul II

Zach Silbernick

"I came that they might have life, and that they might have it more abundantly."

- John 10:10

I write this as I sit here in adoration for the first time since the Coronavirus pandemic started, with my beautiful wife and over two-month-old first-born baby girl. Almost one year ago today, my brother was telling a crowd of almost 500 people on my wedding day, "Zach doesn't date someone often, but when he does, he marries her." You see, I had never had a girlfriend in my life until I was 26, and that girlfriend became my wonderful wife. God bringing us together while I had no experience dating is one of the many miracles He has worked in my life! What I want to share today is how God has blessed my life and worked miracles through three main avenues: Prayer, Adoration, and the Sacraments.

I want to start with prayer. Most of my family and friends know me as a rule follower; some of them have probably been annoyed by how much I follow the rules, but other than a stretch in second grade (Thanks Mrs. Goedderz for setting me straight!), I have always taken great pride in following the rules. So, naturally, when I was told to pray at religion classes, that is what I did. And when I was told to pray for my future spouse, I did that as well. I even listened to my outstanding Confirmation teachers and asked for St. Maria Goretti's intercession for my future wife. I really had no idea at the time what I was doing praying for her intercession, but God worked miracles and continues to work miracles through my imperfect prayers. While I was praying for my future spouse to be a strong Catholic who was chaste, pure, holy, and—let's be honest—good looking, little did I know that she was also doing the same for me. I remember being 24 or 25 years old and doubting whether God would ever answer my prayers. Having no dating experience, how could I ever meet my wife that I was praying for?

Around that time, one of my best friends, a strong Catholic, had invited me over for dinner at his parents' house. His parents' love for God was contagious, and their marriage truly was a sacrament, a sign of God's love to the world. During our conversation that night, they told me something I will never forget: "As we look back on our lives following God's plan for them, they are better than our wildest dreams, better than we ever could have imagined." That truth gave me hope that I would find my future spouse, someone who would run the race toward Heaven with me and be a sacrament of God's love like they were. I held on to that hope even when it seemed like it would never happen, and I continued to pray and trust in God. And even with my lack of dating experience, God brought my beautiful, holy wife and I together through our local Catholic Young Adult group, answering our prayers and blessing us both in more ways than we ever could have imagined. We even ended up getting married on July 6th: the feast day of Saint Maria Goretti! That was one of the many miracles that proved to us the power of prayer in our lives.

We also saw the power of prayer when God worked a miracle to help us buy our first house after we did a rosary walk in the neighborhood we wanted to live in, praying that He would help us to be able to live there if it was His will; I kid you not, a house came on to the market less than a week later right where we had ended the rosary, and our offer was chosen over many others! He also gave us tremendous peace and helped us deliver a healthy, 9lb 12oz baby with no pain medication in the middle of a pandemic, and He has brought countless other blessings, many of which we probably won't even see until we get to Heaven one day. I want to stress just how important prayer has been in my life, but also how much I have struggled, and still struggle, with making prayer a priority in my daily life. You see, I think the devil tries to ruin our days by making us so busy and preoccupied that we don't take time to pray. At least he does that to me. I often fall into the trap of busyness, and I don't take time to pray each day. Thanks be to God, He is so much greater than the devil, and He is so incredibly merciful that even if I go several days without making time for prayer, when I do take that time to start my day off right with prayer in the morning, He is right there waiting for me to turn to Him and choose to love Him again. He never stops loving and blessing me, and when I turn to God in prayer, His blessings never stop pouring out.

Now one would think that as a rule follower, I would never get into trouble. However, this is unfortunately untrue. Sometimes I follow the rules of the world too much. One particular instance was in college. I loved my professors and education that I received from my college, and some of my best friends today I met during college. I even went to a Catholic college, but I found out years after graduating that this college was Catholic in name, but it doesn't follow all of the teachings of the Pope and of the Catholic Church. This would make sense why many of the religious teachings I learned there left me wanting more, almost feeling empty inside. As far as religion goes, they taught a lot about doing what feels best when it comes to religion. They never went deep into the beauty and truth of our Catholic faith, but instead emphasized doing what I thought, or what others thought, felt best when it came to religion. I now realize that I don't want a religion based off of another human being's ideas, even if those ideas are my own. We are humans, and we are flawed. I want the true Faith taught by God Himself, Jesus Christ, carried on today by our spiritual father here on earth, the Pope. Unfortunately, at the time, I bought into this 'what feels good' religion. I started praying only when I felt like it. I never went to adoration because sitting for an hour in silence was never something I felt like doing. Instead I felt like being busy, getting things off my to-do list, and gaining lots of accolades in school and in life. I always felt called to help other people, so I went to college to become a math teacher; however, as school went on, I became so preoccupied with becoming successful that I decided that being a high school math teacher was not prestigious enough for me. So, my senior year, I applied for a Doctoral program in mathematics instead of student teaching. Not only was I accepted, but I was offered an assistantship position so that they would pay for my entire doctoral program! I was so proud of myself; I had my whole life figured out. My plans were falling into place: I would be a doctor in math and teach at a university someday. The problem is that they were my plans, not God's plans.

As my senior year went on, I became very uneasy. Something was wrong, but I couldn't figure out what it was. Why wasn't I happy? This nagging feeling that I wasn't doing what I was called to do became worse and worse until one night I finally fell to my knees in prayer in an act of complete surrender to God's will. In that moment, God made it clear to me I wasn't following His will for my life. He wanted me to help other people, not feed my pride and live for myself. During that prayer time, He made it so clear that I was meant to be a high school math teacher, not a professor of mathematics. The only problem was that I should have started student teaching a month earlier, but I had instead switched to higher-level math courses that would help me in graduate school. There was no way I could switch back to student teaching and still become a teacher that year. Or so I thought. Thankfully, God can make all things possible, and he had blessed me with an amazing math advisor who not only supported my decision, but also helped me switch out of his advanced math courses into a student teaching role. Within a week, I was able to be placed as a student teacher, and I literally finished the 16 required weeks of student teaching on the last day of school, the last possible day to fulfill my student teaching requirement.

Near the end of college, and into my first few years of teaching, my faith quickly fell into just going to Mass on Sundays and then maybe a quick prayer before meals and bed. This led to some rough years of constant busyness and chasing after the very empty things of this world. It wasn't until several years after college when I was sick and tired of constantly being busy or preoccupied with sports, television, or work that I finally went back to adoration, back to receiving the sacrament of confession at least once a month, if not more often, and back to being involved with the Catholic Church beyond just going to Mass on Sundays. When I started to receive confession, dive deeper into my faith, and, most importantly, go to adoration regularly, I finally started to feel fully alive again.

Going back to adoration wasn't easy. If you're anything like me and struggle sitting still for an hour, I highly recommend the book *21 Ways to Worship: A Guide to Eucharistic Adoration* by Vinny Flynn. It is a very easy read, which was good for me, and man it helped tremendously. Adoration made such a difference for me, because I realized that when we are in adoration, God is there and fully present. When I spend time in adoration, I can finally slow down and give all of my worries and fears over to God. He is truly our best friend. He loves us more than anyone else in the world, and we do not have to do anything to earn that love. He loves us as we are right now and wants a life for us that is better than we ever could imagine it to be. For me, knowing that relieves all of the anxieties of the world and reminds me that I am here on this earth for Him. It's a reminder to give up my selfish desires and live for God, and there is something so freeing about that idea. Growing up, I never heard much about adoration; it is almost like this amazing secret of the Catholic Faith. Adoration is where I first encountered God and made my Catholic Faith my own at a Steubenville retreat in early high school, and when I start to falter in my relationship with Him, adoration—spending time with Jesus Himself—always helps me get my life back on track. A story that really put the power of adoration into perspective for me was about a city in northern Mexico called Ciudad Juarez. This town was known as one of the most dangerous cities in the world from 2008 until 2010. They introduced Perpetual Adoration (where Jesus is exposed in the monstrance 24/7) in 2013, and now it is safer than many American Cities, with the murder rate dropping from 3,766 to 256. Just as the introduction of Perpetual Adoration brought new life to that city, spending time in Jesus' presence brings new hope, joy, and abundant life into my life (Knap).

I want to stress the importance of the sacraments in my life as well. Despite all of God's blessings, I still struggle to love God always, and I often waste way too much time on my phone and end up avoiding prayer in the day. I still get caught up in the lies of this world, and I worry about making lots of money and owning material possessions. The Sacrament of Reconciliation gives me the grace to overcome these struggles and live a more virtuous life. I still stumble and fall daily, but through God's grace poured out in this sacrament, I also have daily victories where I choose God above all else.

God also pours out His grace through the sacrament of Holy Matrimony for my wife and I! Through this sacrament, He gives us the grace to die to ourselves, put our own selfish desires away, and to love one another. The Sacrament of Holy Matrimony truly is amazing. The world confuses the word love with infatuation, or 'Disney princess love.' True love is really giving of ourselves, dying to

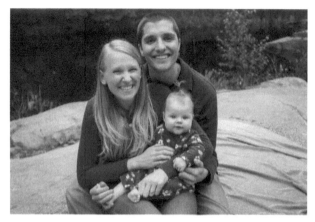 ourselves, and wanting the better for the other person. Naturally, I struggle with my own selfish desires even after marriage, but God's grace helps both my wife and I to die to ourselves and love one another. Not only that, but through the sacrament of Holy Matrimony, God gives my wife and I the grace to love our daughter as well! That grace is especially helpful when she has to be fed at 2am or has a blowout all over her car seat.

The greatest graces, though, come from the Sacrament of the Eucharist. I have been going to Mass my entire life, but there is so much that I didn't understand, and that I am still learning, about the Eucharist. I remember moving to Texas one summer of college for work. I had never left home before, I had no vehicle, and it was difficult being on the other side of the country so far from central Minnesota. However, that first Sunday, I found the nearest church and walked there, and my anxieties from being so far away from family melted away. I remember the church there was under construction, and they had no A/C in the Texas summer heat. The priest explained that the comforts of the Mass shouldn't be our reason for going to church. A good choir, the homily, or even the priest shouldn't be our reason for attending Mass. We should attend Mass to spend time with Jesus and to thank Him for all that He has done for us. If there are things that annoy us about a church, that is just more to offer up to Jesus, to show how thankful we are to Him. Not only did this make me realize how often I would complain about church for silly reasons, but more importantly, this was the first moment I truly understood that the Catholic Mass is, at its foundation, the same everywhere in the world. All around the world there are Catholics celebrating the

Eucharist just like we do. It's funny, my wife knows that I am a homebody and I become anxious when I am far from home, but no matter how far from central Minnesota I travel, I always feel at peace knowing that God and the Mass will be there to make me feel at home.

I remember walking into a church after just moving to a new town about a year before I met my wife. A young priest was explaining the power of the Mass in his homily. He explained that Jesus dying on the cross for our sins, and offering himself up as a living sacrifice for us, is the ultimate act of love. He explained how many people might look at Jesus on the Crucifix and wonder why we would have that featured so prominently in every church. It is because it is a sign of true love. God loved us so much that he suffered on the cross for us, and at every Mass we are brought back to that one sacrifice where Jesus offered Himself up for the salvation of our souls. I will always remember this Mass and to look to the Crucifix as a reminder of how to truly love people as God loves us.

As I mentioned, I am still learning so much about the Mass. There is so much to learn, which I think is what makes it so beautiful. Just the other day, my niece, who is interested in joining the Catholic Church, asked to watch a video called 'The Veil Removed' (https://www.youtube.com/watch?v=OOLZDaTgIaM). It depicts what is going on spiritually at every Mass: how our guardian angels go up as we pray during the Mass, and how our prayers and theirs are united with all of the angels and saints. The video shows how God's love is poured out for us at every Mass. God continues to teach each me the beauty and wonder of the Mass and the Eucharist. It is truly breathtaking.

Prayer, Adoration, and the Sacraments… I cannot stress how powerful these three things have been in my life. I think these three things truly set apart Catholicism from any other religion. I have spent many years just going through the motions of my faith, falling into the lies of this world, doing what feels best, or just turning to God once a week at Mass and then forgetting about Him the rest of the week.

While this led to some high moments, in the long run this way of life left me wanting more, never being fully satisfied. However, when I have made prayer, adoration, and the sacraments pillars in my life, putting my own selfish desires away, God has blessed me abundantly through them. I don't always see those blessings, and sometimes it takes many years to see God's plan come together, but these three things, along with laying down my life for God, have brought true fulfillment and joy to my life. I pray through the intercession of all the saints that my family and I will be given the grace to keep prayer, adoration, and the sacraments as the foundation of our life. I pray that more people in our world do so as well, and I pray that whoever reads this may find more time for prayer, adoration, and the sacraments in their lives, and through these three things and God's grace that they may come to have life, and have it more abundantly.

Knap, P. (n.d.). Mexican City Sees Stunning Drop in Violence as Adoration Increases. Retrieved November 02, 2020, from https://www.ncregister.com/blog/mexican-city-sees-stunning-drop-in-violence-as-adoration-increases

"The first end I propose in our daily work is to do the will of God; second, to do it in the manner He wills it; and thirdly, to do it because it is His will."

-Saint Elizabeth Ann Seton

Shannon Hillestad

"Master, to whom shall we go? You have the words of eternal life."

- John 6:68

The Christian life is a story of continuous conversion. On a daily basis, we must turn back to God after becoming distracted by worldly desires. My initial conversion to Christianity occurred my freshman year of high school. From that day forward, my life was forever changed. However, distractions were more prevalent than ever in college, and I spent a long time away from the Church. Then, almost 10 years after my initial conversion, I experienced a glorious reversion to the church of my youth, the ancient Church which Christ established, the mysterious, imperfect, yet triumphant Catholic Church.

I was blessed to grow up in a lively parish that placed a lot of value on its youth. We had two full-time youth ministers, a praise and worship band, at least two retreats per year, annual mission trips, and weekly bible studies. I came to know the Lord personally my freshman year of high school during adoration and praise and worship on a weekend retreat under the stars in South Georgia. I remember breaking into tears during the song "Better is One Day", overwhelmed by the Love of our Savior. From that night forward, my own desires were lost in the Lord's overpowering desire for my life.

My junior year of high school, I began dating a boy from school. He was handsome, nice and funny. I had concerns because he was not Catholic. But he was Christian, and most importantly, he liked me! It felt good to be wanted. Early on in the relationship, I knew he was not the one for me. Not only was he not Catholic, but he also did not support my Catholic Faith. He would not go to church with me, although I deeply desired for him to. I often went to his church with him as a sort of "compromise"- a compromise that was never reciprocated. Despite my intuition, I stayed with him. After all, I needed a date to the prom. Prom day came and went, and still I stayed. It was nice to have someone with whom I could spend all my time, someone with whom I was comfortable. Months turned into years, and despite several attempts to leave the relationship I always ended up back in the comfort of his arms.

Looking back, it is easy to see the false idol my relationship had become. I selfishly wanted to date someone— anyone— to boost my self-confidence. The feeling of being chosen, liked above others, was so intoxicating that I let myself be swept away by it. I totally immersed myself in this relationship, quick to leave behind all others including my growing relationship with God. I quit going to youth group regularly. In the face of temptation, I compromised the morals that the Church had instilled. Quite simply, my relationship with my boyfriend became my god.

I longed for us to share our faith together. My personal faith felt like a heavy burden that I needed to carry on my own. I had great friends who supported me, but I felt like I needed the support of my boyfriend in order to live the faithful life I desired. However, it was made clear through the years that he would not be swayed toward the Catholic Church. He was full of doubt regarding Church teaching, and I was lacking in adequate explanations. As years went by, his doubts became my own. For me, it began with a hurt and anger that he could not receive the Eucharist. Wouldn't Jesus want to give Himself to everyone, even if they don't believe in Him? Then the doubt crept into every area of Catholic teaching. How can you know Catholic teaching to be trustworthy and true when so much of it is not directly in the Bible? Why so much focus on Mary; isn't that just distracting us from focusing on God? Can't we go to God directly for forgiveness? There is no need for the sacrament of Confession. Why baptize infants? Shouldn't each person make that choice of baptism for himself? The natural progression of my doubts led me to question the validity of my own infant baptism, and in my senior year of undergraduate studies at the University of Georgia, I made the decision to be baptized in the Baptist Church.

The decision did not come lightly and not without opposition from my loving parents. My heart felt so heavy. I wanted to honor God and demonstrate this outward sign of faith. Yet, I felt so sad. The week after I scheduled the baptism, the pastor announced my intent to be baptized in front of the church. I stood in front of the congregation after the service so everyone could greet and encourage me. I felt so foolish because I could not stop crying the whole time. I hoped people would interpret my emotions as tears of joy, but I knew better. I felt sorrowful. I had followed my logic and intellect to this juncture. My head, full of doubt about the Mother Church, felt sure this was the right path. But my heart could do nothing but mourn. Still I followed through with my decision. My boyfriend and I now claimed the same religion; yet, to my surprise, it changed nothing in our relationship. My faith seemed to be no less of a burden, and my boyfriend was no more of a support. Instead of a change in religion, the Lord was calling me to a change of heart. I needed to give the Lord His rightful place as King of my Heart. I needed to give Him full reign.

My second year of graduate school, I was shocked when my boyfriend broke up with me out of the blue. He said, "I don't want to, but I feel like it's what God is calling me to do." My heart broke. I lost my best friend, the man I thought I would marry. Yet, simultaneously, my heart cried out, "Thank you, Jesus!" For He freed me from my sin. I was set free from this relationship I had idolized for so long. I was free to return wholeheartedly to the Lord. Several months after our split, I cracked open a book entitled "Born Fundamentalist, Born again Catholic." My mother had given it to me a year or so earlier. I remember laughing when I received it, thinking, *"Let it go, Mom."* Thank God a mother's love is relentless.

The book is written by a former Evangelical pastor David B. Currie. He grew up in a Fundamentalist home. Both his parents were biblical scholars. He studied in the Masters of Divinity program at Trinity Evangelical Divinity School. I was inspired by Currie because his heart was fully committed to following truth wherever it may lead. His conversion to the Catholic Faith was anything but easy. He lost many friends and even relationships with family members. Yet once he was convinced of where the truth lie, he felt he had no choice but to pursue it. When asked what led to his conversion, Currie's simple answer was, "Scripture." When I first read this statement in the introduction of the book, I was floored. I had come to believe that Catholic teaching was nowhere to be found in the Bible.

When asked what brought me back to the Catholic Faith, I always mention this book. Yet a more pointed answer comes in Chapter 2: "Communion and the Real Presence." Currie goes in depth studying the second half of John Chapter 6, in which Jesus says,

"Amen, amen, I say to you unless you eat the flesh of the Son of Man and drink his blood, you do not have life within you. Whoever eats my flesh and drinks my blood has eternal life, and I will raise him on the last day. For my flesh is true food, and my blood is true drink."

Jesus is clear. His Body is true food, His Blood true drink. The thought brings tears to my eyes. What a mysterious, humbling, and beautiful sacrifice. Our Lord has given Himself to us, fully and completely, in a piece of bread and a cup of wine. He is available to us in a real, physical way at every Mass and in every tabernacle and adoration chapel. Just as the Eucharist led to my first conversion on retreat in high school almost 10 years earlier, it again led me back to the Savior. The Eucharist continues to lead me back to the Lord at Mass every Sunday and every time I visit the chapel. As Currie explains, the Eucharist "feeds our souls" and strengthens us against temptation. How true these words ring in my own life!

The Lord is the master in creating beauty from our sinfulness. My time spent away from the Church was not time totally wasted. Since my reversion, I have come to truly accept my Catholic Faith as my own. I have a much deeper understanding of Catholic teaching and more faithfulness in following the Church's teachings. The answers to many of my doubts have been revealed to me over time. Some are still being revealed. Yet, wherever my doubts still lie, I have learned to surrender to the wisdom of the Spirit that moves through His Bride the Church.

Moreover, I have grown to understand our Protestant brothers and sisters more deeply. I have grown to know that we have more in common than different, and I more deeply desire unity in the greater church. I pray sincerely with Christ that we may all be one (John

17:20). May the Lord in His infinite mercy continue to call us all to Truth and conversion of heart day after day!

Michael Haney

"I am the vine, you are the branches. He who abides in me, and I in him, he it is that bears much fruit, for apart from me you can do nothing."

-John 15:5 RSV

Everyone has a unique path to walk and their own story to write. God calls us all according to His plan. To judge your path against another's would rob you of becoming all that God created you to be. Wherever you are on your path, or whatever is behind you, know that you are never lost from God. Be open and available for His plan, and simply say "yes" to whatever He asks of you. Do this and your life will be more fruitful than you could ever imagine. John 15:5 is one of my favorite verses and a huge part of my story, for the closer I have been to the Lord, the more fruitful my life has been. Some people are called by God in a particular moment or event. Others he whispers to, which can easily be lost in the noise and distraction of the world today. Like drops in the bucket, over time they will fill you up and help you become who you are supposed to be. I don't know where God is leading me or what marvelous plans He has in store for my life, but I am His and that is all that I need to know to be at peace. This is the story of my path and how I got to where I am today.

My story is one of those that takes place throughout my life. There was no single moment where I was shown the light and was saved; it happened little by little. I find myself looking back and seeing it as different levels of intimacy with God. Some seasons of my life were really tough and some have been filled with amazing joy, but all of them have been blessed by God in their own way.

I grew up in a broken home where my parents had been divorced when I was just two years old. Before I can even remember, both my parents had remarried. I lived with my mom through the school year and with my dad in the summer months. My sister and I were children from the first marriage, while my three half-brothers were blessings from my mom's second marriage. We were raised Lutheran and went to church on a pretty regular basis. Besides going to church on Sundays and attending Wednesday school, I was a Boy Scout which met in our church basement. I was at our church a lot growing up, and I have some very fond memories. I liked to volunteer and take part in services. I was always one of the loudest singers, even though I was never on-key or completely knew the words! I was just a kid and never took anything too seriously, as my life was always changing. As soon as I got used to something, seasons would change and I was off to Dad's house for the summer and life would begin again. In the summer months, we would not see the inside of the church unless we were with our grandparents or I was off to scout camp where we met at the church before departing. I never took the time to create roots or to get to know God on a deeper level, as I was more concerned with friends and activities to keep my mind off how tough things could be from time to time.

I had my first introduction to Catholicism through some new neighbors we had when we moved to Alexandria. They were the Koeps, an amazing family with a girl who was a year older than me. I was probably somewhere between 10-12 years old when I met them. Their daughter Kayla and I became instant friends, and I quickly became like part of their family. I think her parents could see some of the struggles that our family was going through, and they treated me as a son. I was often invited to dinner where I remember Harold (Kayla's dad) leading prayer before every meal. I could tell that there was something special about this family. Their faith and love were a huge blessing, not only to me, but so many others in our community. However, it was only a couple of years until Kayla and her family moved out of town and another chapter of life started.

High school was a very dark time in my life, as my mom and stepdad were going through a tough divorce. My mom and real dad couldn't get along in any way, shape, or form. My sister, who had always been there to be with me, had gotten married at 18 and was off to college with a new husband and baby. I hated to be at home, and I did just about anything to avoid being there by staying at friends' houses and going on as many school trips as possible. Thankfully, the Boy Scouts was full of opportunities to go camping- a place where I found lots of joy! Once I even disappeared for a Thanksgiving weekend without letting my parents know, inviting myself to one of my friend's family Thanksgiving celebrations. I did whatever I could to avoid being home at all costs.

After graduating from High School, I found myself diving into work full time. I worked for Pizza Hut at the time and would for 14 years. I never had aspirations of college or felt a certain career calling, so I dove into work, picking up as many shifts as possible and learning the ins and outs of restaurant life. Within three years, I was the general manager of the Alexandria location, and it wasn't long before I was running a second location, in various locations around the state depending on the year. It was a life of labor and not much else. I would be working 60-75 hours per week and was off to the bar to hide during my off times.

It was during this time that I met Trista. She, too, was from a broken home, and we had a lot in common as we were both trying to get through life as best we could. We had an on-again, off-again relationship for years, and at some point she decided to go to cosmetology school in Saint Cloud. We dated the entire time she went to school, living separate lives for the most part and only seeing each other on weekends. Somewhere during it all, Trista's faith started to blossom. She started to take me to Mass, and I could feel something special there. I remember being so excited to bless myself with the holy water when entering the church. I did not want to give up my Lutheran church, as it was all I knew, so we had agreed to go to my church every other week as well. Things looked like they could get better for both of us.

During this, my sister Julie was a huge help. By this point, her family was thriving, as was her marriage and faith. She was always there to support me as much as she could. I remember her asking me one day, "If you got to heaven, what would you tell God you did with your life?" Wow, talk about a gut punch! All I could say was that I ran a good restaurant. I didn't want that to be the only piece of my life that I was remembered for. After many months of restlessness, I decided to move to St. Cloud and go to the Technical College. Trista and I would be moving in together and trying to start a life together.

Somewhere along the line, we decided it was the next logical thing to get married; after all, we had been together for years and were living together. We figured that we might as well have the paper that says we belong together. This is when things started to change and seeds were planted that would change my life forever. We started to only attend Catholic Mass on the weekends, as I didn't have a church in St. Cloud, and we started marriage preparation with Fr. Mike Kellogg. What an amazing priest! It wasn't until one weekend when Trista's grandparents were housing a priest at their farm that things really got started. I spent hours getting to know him, and the Faith he shared seemed so interesting. This led me to working with Fr. Mike to become Catholic. I spent almost a year meeting with Fr. Mike one-on-one learning the faith. This amazing priest was captivating and lived with a love for the Lord that would have anyone asking, "How can I get some of that?" Two weeks before Trista and I got married, I was confirmed Catholic. Oddly enough, I was confirmed Catholic in a Lutheran church! Yup, you read that right- I was confirmed Catholic in a Lutheran church. The Catholic church in Upsala was under construction, so we were celebrating Mass at the Lutheran church down the street. During this time, we had also found St. Anthony's parish in St. Cloud and we really liked attending Mass there. I was starting to burn with this newfound faith, and things were coming together in life. I remember one moment in particular during my RCIA journey of becoming Catholic where I knew I was heading in the direction God wanted me to be. I was in St. Louis with my college DECA group, and I knew that I was going to have to find Mass on my own. I walked all over the city looking for a Catholic Church, and I finally found the Cathedral. I looked up the Mass times and then made a plan to sneak away from my group to go. At this point, I was not public about my faith. On my way to Mass, I remember being so incredibly nervous. What would these people think of me? What would happen if they found out I was not Catholic? I did the only thing I could: I prayed that God would help me through this Mass. I got an answer almost immediately. Walking into this Cathedral was amazing. It was my first experience in a Cathedral, and I was in awe. As I entered, I was welcomed by an usher and I took a seat in the back. He then came over to me and asked if I would bring the gifts forward for Mass. I quickly said that I wasn't Catholic, but he smiled and said, "I don't think that matters," and I had the job. Wow, talk about a prayer answered. Here I was, afraid, and I had one of the most welcoming moments of my life by the Church. You might think I would had given everything after that!

Trista and I got married, and not much changed. We had lived together for years and had given each other ourselves physically prior to our marriage. The only thing that changed was her last name and the fact that we were legally together. We were Sunday Catholics as we went to Mass pretty much every Sunday, but that was all for me. I think Trista's faith was stronger, but we never really talked about it. We continued life the way it had been when we were dating. We pretty much lived separate lives and only spent a day or two a week together as a married couple. A lot of the time, one of us wasn't even home for days at a time. Looking back, I am saddened and embarrassed at how badly I treated her. Everything else came first: work, school, money, and friends. I just assumed she would always be there. I guess we both had just given in to the idea of marriage, but we really didn't know or understand what it takes to be married. I see now that I was not willing to make the sacrifices to put her and our marriage first. She ended up leaving, and she found a good man who treated her right.

Divorce is awful. It doesn't matter if you are in a bad marriage; it still kills you. Growing up, the one and only thing I wanted to be was a dad, and now I had to watch my ex-wife start a family with someone else. I hit a new low. I remember hurting so much and being so mad at myself that I wanted to die from time to time. I thought that is what I deserved. During all of this, people would always try to cheer me up by talking badly about my ex, but that is never helpful. We were both just not ready to commit to doing what you need to do in a marriage to make things work. It took many years and the annulment process for me to heal and to realize how wrong we were together. When I think about that time in my life, I think about a quote from Fr. Tom Knobloch: "Sin doesn't stop Gods plan; it just makes the journey longer and harder." I pray for Trista and her family to this day; I hope she has found all the joy and love she deserves.

One of my friends even urged me, now she was out of my life, that I did not have to be Catholic any more. The thing he didn't understand is that I didn't *have* to be Catholic. I *chose* to be Catholic. I continued to go to St. Anthony's after the divorce, and it was there at that little parish that God really started to take center stage in my life. There are more people there that have helped me on my journey than I could ever mention in this story, and I am so blessed to have every one of them in my life. One person that I have to say has had a huge impact on my life is Helen Ryan (now Helen Theilen). Helen saw something special in me and urged me to become a greeter at one of the doors for Sunday Mass. Reluctantly, I started to greet week after week, and I slowly got to know the parishioners. I even decided to officially become a member of the parish after some time of greeting. Next, Helen nominated me to be on the pastoral council. Step by step, she and other members got me to serve the parish in one way or another. I thought I was doing them a favor, but it turns out the more you serve the more you get in return. As I was taking steps towards God, He was making my life bear more and more fruit. Things were amazing, but I was on a plateau as far as my relationship with God. As a convert it was (or is?) hard to ask questions or to ask others to explain something they mention after Mass when you don't fully understand. After all, I was supposed to be Catholic, and my year of RCIA should have taught me everything I needed to know, right?

Once I started to give my life to Christ more and more, I had gone through the annulment process (which was a huge part of my healing!), I had my first confession (which was terrifying as I was around 30 years old and had a lot of sins to confess!), healing had happened and I had a solid new church family, I started to think about that yearning to be a husband and father again. At some point, my sister Julie again stepped in with a book called "The Old Fashioned Way." This book talks about how dating should actually be courting. If your end goal is to be married, then your entire relationship should be leading up to that point. I dove into the book and started to work on being the kind of man God created me to be, the kind that would make a good husband.

As I started learning what it means to be a worthy husband, people from the parish started to look for a spouse for me. I went on a few dates here and there, with the intention that I would be courting. I had a lot of interesting conversations and got to know some outstanding women, but none were that one that God called me to be with. One day in late spring, my friend Sarah brought her roommate to Mass and introduced us. We both said "hi" but took little notice of each other, then it was off to work for me, and I didn't think too much about this beautiful woman I had just met.

Flash forward to August, I had given one night to loneliness and started an online account on a dating website. It turns out that Katie had also started an account within days of me starting mine. After messaging her and totally missing where we had met before, we started talking. I was open and honest with her from the start, explaining my understanding of courting vs. dating. Within a week we decided to meet, and it was an amazing date over coffee. I remember her faith shining through every part of her. I found a deeper level of faith in Katie than I had ever known. She was also willing to help me learn, and I could ask questions. On our fourth date we went to the Grasshopper Chapel in Cold Spring, and she asked me to pray the rosary with her. I said yes, even though I was scared and did not really know the prayers. After praying and having my eyes closed for the entire time, I opened them to see the words of the Hail Mary written on granite right in front of my face as we prayed. It felt like God saying, "If you trust Me, I will take care of you." I knew right then and there that this was the one I was supposed to be with.

With the help of Katie and her family, my faith has blossomed. One of the biggest changes came from her bringing me to Adoration and making it a weekly part of our relationship. I had never even heard of Eucharistic Adoration until I met Katie. I will never forget the night I left the hospital to go to our Holy Hour after our first daughter, Mariana, was born. It was one of my first days as a father, and there I was in front of the Blessed Sacrament asking for direction and strength. Katie's parents and family members were also a huge influence, always supporting and guiding me. The day I met her dad

(Gary) and brother-in-law (Steven), I was going to a Newman Center benefit where Katie was hosting a table. After her parents found out that I was going, their schedule quickly cleared up and they were able to come as well. Anyway, I agreed to ride to the dinner with Gary and Steven, and I found out that Fr. Jeremy Ploof would be joining us as well. So there I was with my girlfriend's dad, brother-in-law, and priest. The night was going to be interesting! The drive down to the dinner was one I will never forget. I sat in the back seat with Fr. Jeremy and he pretty much asked me my entire life story. What a better way for a dad to get to know the man their daughter is dating than have a priest ask questions in the back seat of a car for an hour and a half. I questioned in my mind if this was the plan all along.

I courted Katie for a short time before we decided to get married. We met in August and started dating in September, and by Christmas we were engaged! This time we waited until we were married to live together and we gave ourselves to each other fully on our wedding night. What an amazing gift. Preparing to be married came with some stresses. I had not given Trista the time and attention she deserved or wanted, and I decided I would not make that same mistake now. Because of this and knowing Katie's primary love language was quality time, I decided to leave my job that I had been at for seven and a half years. I loved my job, having the feel of family from my boss, and it was very secure and could allow me to provide for us. Nevertheless, I knew that I loved Katie and I would do anything to be the husband she deserved and wanted.

My life with Katie had the Lord at the center from the beginning, and we have had more blessings than we can count. We are now expecting our third child and have a beautiful home with a little land that we call home. Between then and now we have both switched jobs twice and purchased and sold a home. Life has been moving quickly, with the Lord opening doors and blessing us faster than we could have planned. Together we just keep saying "yes" when we feel God is calling us to something. We have had our struggles, but it is the greatest feeling to have a wife like Katie whom I always know will be there with me through whatever life brings. Sharing our faith with each other and with our kids has strengthened our family immensely as we strive to come closer and closer to God.

My life has been a series of ups and downs, and I have done things wrong and I have done things right, but I have learned a lot. My best advice that I can give is to trust God and do whatever it takes to know Him on the deepest level you can. Don't be afraid to ask questions and to learn. Court your significant other and, in that, save yourself for marriage. I know it is hard, as I have done it both ways, but I promise the gift you give your spouse is greater than you can imagine. John 15:5 is a good image of my life, as it has never let me down. The closer I am to Christ, the more I am pruned and the more fruit my life bears. May the Lord bring all of us close to Him and make each of our lives abundantly fruitful!

Fr. Andrew Vogel

"Find your delight in the Lord who will give you your heart's desire. Commit your way to the Lord; trust in him and he will act."

- Psalm 37:4-5

My story of God's mercy begins when I was one year old. Why? Because that's when I was found on the doorstep of the police station in Mokpo, a harbor town right on the southwest tip of South Korea. No one knows how or why I ended up there. Sometimes I think I was left there by a teenage unwed mother, but I have no proof of that. At this point, only God knows. Even me being on that doorstep was God's mercy. I can only imagine how hard it was for my mother to leave me there. Yet she did. And thus begins an amazing journey, all orchestrated by God and our Blessed Mother Mary.

After that I was put in an orphanage. My parents, Bill and Mary Kay Vogel, were the next instruments of God's mercy in my life. They had heard about me from a friend and after thinking and praying about it, they decided to adopt. I'm what they got. I was two and a half when I arrived in the spring of 1977. My parents and my older sister, Gretchen, picked me up from the airport in Minneapolis, Minnesota and drove me back to Ames, Iowa. I have been told I ate grapes all the way home and pointed out every semi-truck. I was then adopted again, this time into the Catholic Church through baptism. I was such a hit that my parents adopted two more from South Korea in the fall of 1978. Finally, on one of the coldest days I can remember, my youngest sister was born in January of 1982. Growing up, I remember feeling close to God, but I don't remember any specific profound moments. My sacramental journey was similar to most any other cradle Catholic. In second grade I received my First Reconciliation. In third grade I had my First Eucharist. In tenth grade I received the sacrament of Confirmation. Even though I went to Catholic elementary school, the priesthood never crossed my mind. In some ways, I don't know why. We had great priests. For a while I even thought priests were perfect. I don't know how my mom brainwashed us, but I grew up "knowing" that guns (even toy guns), tattoos, smoking, and motorcycles were evil. So after Mass one Sunday, when I was about ten, I saw Father smoking a cigarette after Mass. It was right then and there that my belief that priests were perfect ended. Shortly after Confirmation, my faith hit an all-time low. I was very close to being an atheist. I remember specifically one day during my junior year of high school, sitting in choir[1] and hearing the girl behind me say something to the effect that the only purpose of religion is to be kind to one another and one doesn't need religion to do that.[2] At the time, and in quite a few ways, this made a lot of sense to me. Since I was a nerd, I was also reading A Brief History of Time by Stephen Hawkins, which supported the idea that God was basically unnecessary.

During the fall of 1994, I went off to college at Iowa State University... which is in Ames, Iowa. Even though I went to college in my hometown, my parents made me live in the dormitory. They wanted me to have the "full" college experience. When I started college, I would say my faith was still on the rebound. By the mercy and grace of God, right from the start I made Sunday Mass a habit. Later in my freshman year, I was also introduced to another Christian group on campus, The Salt Company, better known as TSC. TSC was a "non-denominational" ministry put on by Southern Baptists. Immersed in the TSC ministry and culture, I felt God calling me to spend more than just an hour a week developing my relationship with Him. It was with friends that I made at TSC that I learned how to make Christ a part of my daily life. I learned through positive peer pressure to let Christ affect what music I listened to, what TV shows I watched, what movies I saw. It might have been a little too overbearing, but it was what I needed at that time to get rid of the filth that had crept into my life. I also began to read the Bible every day and get involved in Bible studies. It was in this fundamentalist Christian culture that I learned the basics of being a Christian, of being a follower of Christ, of being a disciple.

For the next couple of years, I continued to be involved at TSC and went to Mass on Sunday at the Catholic Newman Center. Some Sundays I would go to the TSC Sunday service in the morning and then 7 PM Mass at the Catholic Newman Center. All-in-all, by the fall of my junior year I was involved in about seven different Christ-centered activities a week between TSC and the Newman Center. During my junior year, I did an internship at IBM during the spring and summer semesters of 1997 in Rochester, Minnesota. I was a little apprehensive about moving to Rochester because I knew that the support system would not be there, at least not to the same degree it was at Iowa State. So before I left, I mentioned to friend that I believed that God might be calling me to start a Bible study in Rochester. This friend introduced me to a strong Christian from TSC named Jeff Owens who was also interning at IBM over the next seven months.

However, once I arrived, that call to start a Bible Study for interns was put on the back burner in the midst of making lots of new friends and trying to get used to my new surroundings. The first week I was there I did try to find a young adult Catholic Christian group, but I didn't find a thing. So I just pushed the idea to the back of my mind. Besides, after a couple of weeks I was already deeply entrenched in other social activities. As the weeks wore on, though, I felt further and further from God. I wasn't doing anything that necessarily detracted from my relationship with God, but these activities certainly weren't helping that relationship grow.

So after a month or so into the internship, I gave the TSC guy a call, Jeff Owens. Jeff said he was still up for starting a Bible study. So I sent an email to all 150 or so IBM co-ops. We only got five people to reply, and two of them were Jeff's roommates. I was disappointed in the small number of people, but God used this humble start so that His glory would be better displayed. Jeff Owens was an awesome Bible study leader. Under his guidance we all learned a lot about living a Christian life. Even so, for most of the spring the group size remained at seven.

Another thing I did to get closer to God was to go on some retreats back in Iowa through the Newman Center and TSC. I especially remember the TSC retreat. I knew God was calling me to give my whole self, my whole life, to Him. However, as a scientist and an engineer, I always felt like I had to know one more thing. I was actually jealous of people who could just give themselves to Christ. One of the leaders challenged me and asked me, what sin was keeping me from giving my life to Christ? He quoted me Romans 6:23: "For the wages of sin is death, but the gift of God is salvation through Jesus Christ our Lord." I went for a walk by myself in the dark. I couldn't think of any such sin, so finally I just gave Jesus my pride. The fact that I couldn't think of any sin shows just how sinful my heart was. But there, kneeling in a dirt path somewhere in central Iowa, I gave my life to Christ for the first time. Now, there have been times that I've taken it back since. This cycle of giving my life to Christ and me taking it back has happened countless times and continues to happen. God our Father is so very patient with us. He takes us back as many times as we give ourselves back to Him. Knowledge can only take us so far. At some point we have to take the leap of faith. Not a faith that contradicts reason, but a faith into knowledge beyond reason.

Back to the internship Bible Study. During the summer, we added some more members. One week had over twenty people there.[3] One of these new interns and members of our Bible study was a young, vivacious, joyful, energetic woman from Taylor University. She was a strong fundamentalist Christian. She was beautiful not just on the outside, but truly on the inside. Not just Christian guys, but all guys were attracted to her. She was attractive inside and out. I got her to go on a date with me after I hit her with a tennis ball as we were playing tennis.[4] She and others from the Bible study continued to challenge me.

One area that I had been feeling challenged more and more on is why I was still Catholic. By this time, in some ways I was sick of the whole denomination question. I felt torn. The dark side of Christian denominationalism, this war for the ages, was being fought right in my own heart and I was no longer a willing participant. It got to the point where I had no clue what God was calling me to do. There were seriously times when I wanted to give up on religion, give up on Christianity, just so I could have some peace in my soul. But I also knew this would mean denying that Christ died on the cross for my sins. This much I knew was true. But beyond that, I didn't know what to believe. Sometimes during the summer at the Rochester Bible studies, Catholicism would not fair very well.

Towards the end of the summer, toward the end of our internship, this young energetic woman from Taylor University (we'll call her Kelly...since that's what her name is) one evening forcefully, but lovingly, questioned my Catholic faith, questioned why I was still Catholic. It was true. I had been feeling this tension between the Catholic faith I grew up with and the fundamentalist Christianity I was deeply invested in at TSC for quite some time. After hanging out with my friends at TSC for a couple of years, I now knew what fundamentalist Christians believe, why they believe it, and how to defend those teachings with the Bible. After going to Catholic elementary school and CCD through 12th grade, I knew what Catholics believed, but I didn't know why, and I definitely could not defend the Catholic Church's teachings in the Bible. So Kelly spent a couple of hours with me going over all the ways fundamentalist Christians are right and Catholics are wrong. After talking to her, I was ready to call my parents and tell them that I no longer wanted to be Catholic. And that would have been fine with my parents. See, even though all of us kids received our Sacraments in the Catholic Church, we would go every other weekend to my dad's Lutheran church. The Lutheran Church had way better donuts and Kool-Aid after Sunday service than the Catholic Church did. So my parents would have been more than okay with me leaving the Catholic Church. But I ended up not making that call. Instead, I started reading a book a friend's mother gave me. The book was Rome Sweet Home by Scott and Kimberly Hahn.

So as I transitioned back to campus life for the fall of my fourth year of college, I continued to consume every Catholic apologetics book I could find: Jeff Cavin, Steven Ray, David Curry, Karl Keating, and others. Father Jon Seda, the chaplain at Iowa State University's Newman Center, gave a talk titled: "How Catholics Differ From Other Christians." At the talk I met two other young men who also wanted to learn more about Catholics apologetics. I honestly don't know how I got my homework done that fall semester of my fourth year of college. After three months of intensive reading and talking with others, I become convinced, I knew, that the Catholic Church, and she alone, had the fullness of Truth, the preserved Deposit of Faith given by Jesus to the Apostles.

Once I knew that the Catholic Church had the fullness of truth, the Deposit of Faith, I quit going to the TSC events and became fully invested in the St. Thomas Aquinas Newman Center. I guess I hung around too much, because later that fall semester Father Jim asked if I had ever considered being a priest. I honestly answered, "No." He then told me that a priest discernment group met every Sunday evening and said he thought I should join. I told him, "No, thanks." However, a week later, he asked me again. This time he said they serve pizza at these meetings. I told him, "I'll be there."

Towards the end of the first semester of my fourth year of college, there was an evening where I didn't have much homework to do and I was kind of tired, as most college students are. So I decided to go to bed at 7 o'clock. I wanted to sleep, but God wanted to reveal another calling to me. So as I was lying there, some things were going through my mind. I had enjoyed my internship in Rochester the semester and summer before, but I felt like God was calling me to do something that more directly improved people's lives. There is nothing immoral with making faster computers, but I felt like God was calling me personally to something that more directly benefited people. As I laid there in bed, I asked the Lord about becoming a doctor or a psychiatrist. But God didn't seem to be going in that direction. I even brought up the dreaded priesthood question, but God didn't even seem to be leading me in that direction. Finally it came to me that I could use my engineering for medical purposes. This would more directly impact people's lives and use my engineering skills. To make a long story short, Iowa State University did not have a biomedical engineering undergrad program. So over my last semesters in college I took human anatomy and organic chemistry. This is where God seemed to be leading me. So when I started my job hunting, I started with Guidant and Medtronic, both biomedical engineering companies that make pacemakers and other such medical devices. Eventually I ended up back in Rochester, MN, working for the famous Mayo Clinic. My specific job was to offer computer support for the Radiation Oncology Department.

Life was going well. I enjoyed my job and had great co-workers. I dated a beautiful, amazing Catholic nurse that had gone to school at Franciscan University of Steubenville, OH. I even bought a house with a twenty year-mortgage. I also got involved in faith formation and the youth group at my parish.

About a year into my job, I was involved in a Bible study on Revelations which was led by a young associate priest at the parish named Father Andrew Beerman. I remember waiting after class one day, needing a Confession. There was another woman waiting for Father Beerman, wanting to ask him a question. So I asked her what her question was. I don't remember what it was, but I gave the best answer I could using the Catholic apologetics I had learned. When Father Beerman became available, the woman got to ask her question. Father basically gave the same answer I did. At which point, the woman turned to me and asked if I had ever thought about being priest. In my head, my answer was, "NOOOOOOOO!!!! Lord, we already discussed this, and I am not called to the priesthood, right?" She also suggested I get a spiritual director. So as a result of this incident, I did not enter seminary, but I did get a spiritual director.

I must have hung around the church too much, because over the next five years, others approached me and asked if I had ever considered the priesthood. I always say my Vocation started from without instead of from within. The priesthood was not something I thought of on my own. In fact, on my own, I had other plans for my life. However, enough people were bold enough to ask me if I had ever considered the priesthood. I also would go on youth trips where they would have an altar call for vocations. I would stand in the back as a chaperone, looking cool, but these questions finally got to me. One thing that really helped was that my spiritual director said that seminary is not the place where you go when you are sure you will become a priest, but a place to further discern the priesthood. Through this idea, and through much prayer, much discernment, and much agony, I finally agreed that God was calling me to the seminary. I didn't know if I was called to the priesthood, but I knew I was called to the seminary. I had talked to a couple of older men who said they too had thought about the priesthood, but had never done anything about it. These men were happily married with kids. It crossed my mind that I would never want to do that to a woman. I would never want to spend my married life wondering if I had been called to the priesthood. So from the time the priest first mentioned the priesthood to me and me finally entering the seminary, seven years elapsed. I went to Winona in the fall of 2004, to Immaculate Heart Seminary on the campus of St. Mary's University thinking that I would put in my time, maybe get kicked out in three or four months, then move on with my life, get married, have kids, grow old, die, and not look back.

Obviously that didn't happen. The six years of seminary were not easy. I continued to discern and learn more about God, about prayer, and about myself. At Sacred Heart Major Seminary in Detroit, where I did major seminary, I was struggling to do 60 minutes of silent prayer a day, something we were expected to do. I was talking to my spiritual director, and he said, "Andy, nobody is a morning person. Just get up and do it." So that's what I do even now. No matter when my day starts, I just get up an hour earlier to spend time with God. However, I do disagree with my spiritual director in that there are such things as morning persons. These people are extremely annoying.

Back in 2004, even before I started seminary, some people brought up the priest scandals that had come to light in Boston in the early 2000s. I told them the scandals were not a reason not to go into the priesthood, but a reason *to* go into the priesthood. Not to be arrogant, but by the mercy of God and humility, I saw myself as part of generation of priests that would change things.

For me, again, being a seminarian was not easy. In some ways, being a priest is not easy either, but in some ways it is. I did not love being a seminarian, but I love being a priest. I say this because if there are any discouraged seminarians out there, hang in there. Priesthood is not the same as being a seminarian. Being the face and presence of God to those around us is an experience that cannot be put into words.

To make a long story short, there is something called candidacy, which is a step towards priesthood. My seminarian classmates and I were going to the public audience with Pope Benedict XVI in Vatican City, in Rome, Italy, and we were allowed to wear clerics, priest shirts, to the audience with the pope. On the way there, a woman stopped me, in a distressed voice, speaking to me in Italian. I still don't know what she wanted, but I knew she saw the collar and wanted a priest. But I was not a priest yet, and I could not give her what she wanted. This made a huge impact on me. A priest is never his own person. In some ways, no one cares about Andrew Vogel any more. But they do care about Father Andrew Vogel. They care that I, 'in persona Christi,' in the person of Christ, am present among them. What a huge responsibility! One that I cannot do on my own. Only by the grace of God do I partially succeed.

When we were in seminary, we would ask priests what is the best part of being a priest, they would often say the Mass, changing bread and wine into the Body, Blood, Soul, and Divinity of Jesus. But for most, a close second was Confessions. I always thought, "How is hearing people's sins, their garbage, a great part of being a priest?" However, sitting on the other side, the priest's side, you quickly realize that Confession isn't primarily about sins, but about God's mercy. I would get mad before I was a priest when I would confess something I thought was a horrible sin and the priest would give me three Hail Marys as a penance. What?! It made no sense. But it does. We cannot even begin to make up for our sins. That's why Christ died on the Cross for us. The penance is there not to make up for anything, but as a first step back to a life of holiness and striving for sainthood.

In the end, it is miracles building on miracles. Remember, I should not be alive. I was born with a heart defect. Remember, I should not be in America. I was found on the doorstep of the police station in Mokpo, South Korea and then adopted and raised in America. Remember, I should not be a Christian, but I fell in with a group in college that took being a disciple of Jesus Christ seriously. Remember, I should not be a Catholic because I almost left the Catholic Church because I had never been taught that the Bible, history, and logic show that the Catholic Church, the only denomination that has existed since the time of Christ, has the fullness of Truth, the Deposit of Faith, given to Jesus Christ to the first bishops, the Apostles. I am eternally thankful to our modern-day Catholic apologists. Remember, I should not be a priest. I had other plans for my life. It wasn't until I was a senior in college that the idea even came up.

My life, my priesthood is a living miracle. I love being a priest. Now, don't get me wrong. There are tough days where I daydream about being in a different Vocation. But ninety-nine percent of the time, there is nothing else I would rather be, would rather do. It is purely by God's mercy that I'm a Catholic priest. God is good. All the time.

---

[1] It is kind of amazing I was in choir since I'm not really allowed to sing in public.

[2] The girl is partially correct; one doesn't need religion to be kind to people. There are a lot of kind atheists in the world. The primary purpose of the Christian religion is Jesus Christ and our relationship to Him. The "rules" are not the primary purpose, but the "rules" flow out of our relationship with Jesus Christ.

[3] The Bible study continued after we left in August. In fact, the Bible study continued for over a year. It got shut down when someone complained that the business email system was being used for something religious. When I look back on the whole thing, the power and guidance of the Holy Spirit is so very apparent.

[4] Take this for what it's worth. I cannot guarantee that hitting someone with a tennis ball will get you a date. Also, it's good to remember that even though I got a date after hitting her with a tennis ball, I am a priest.

Further Reading

Don't miss out on the first two books of the series!

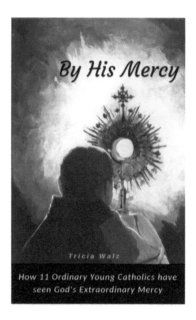

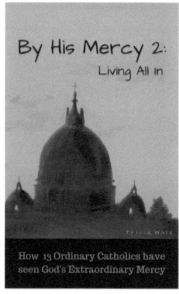

"There is no evil to be faced that Christ does not face with us. There is no enemy that Christ has not already conquered. There is no cross to bear that Christ has not already born for us, and does not now bear with us."

-Saint John Paul II